MORE OF THE
H✦LY
SPIRIT

How to Keep the
Fire Burning in Our Hearts

SR. ANN SHIELDS, SGL

MORE OF THE HOLY SPIRIT

HOW TO KEEP THE FIRE BURNING IN OUR HEARTS

SR. ANN SHIELDS, SGL

the WORD among us® Press

Published by The Word Among Us Press
7115 Guilford Drive, Suite 100
Frederick, Maryland 21704
www.wau.org

17 16 15 14 13   1 2 3 4 5

ISBN: 978-1-59325-229-8
eISBN: 978-1-59325-451-3

Cover design by John Hamilton Designs
Cover image Art Resource

Made and printed in the United States of America

Library of Congress Control Number: 2013940541

Contents

Introduction / 7

1. Come, Holy Spirit! / 11

2. Where Are We Now? / 21

3. The Call to Discipleship / 33

4. Keep the Fire Burning / 49

5. Coming to Know the True God / 65

6. Activating the Gifts of Baptism and Confirmation / 81

7. Three More Gifts: Faith, Hope, and Love / 105

8. "Put On the Whole Armor of God" / 119

9. A Call to Repentance / 129

Conclusion / 135

Appendix:
  General Audience of Pope John Paul II,
    September 6, 1989 / 142
  Regina Caeli of Pope Benedict XVI,
    May 11, 2008 / 149

Bibliography / 153

Endnotes / 154

Introduction

I sense that the moment has come to commit all of the Church's energies to a new evangelization and to the mission ad gentes [to all people]. No believer in Christ, no institution of the Church can avoid this supreme duty: to proclaim Christ to all peoples.

—Pope John Paul II [1]

How do we equip ourselves to meet the challenges of our age? We have been baptized and confirmed. We have received all the gifts intended by God to make us followers and disciples of Jesus Christ. And we know that our "supreme duty" is to evangelize others, to bring them into a life-giving relationship with our heavenly Father through the power of the Holy Spirit.

Yet we also know that we have seen an almost cataclysmic decline of faith in God, especially here in our country and in the Western world. Pope Benedict XVI, who has commented on this decline, wrote this before becoming pope: "For the near future we see the process of secularization continuing; we see the faith diminishing; we see a separation between the commonly accepted culture and Christian faith and culture." [2]

Back in 1967, with the outpouring of the Holy Spirit at Duquesne University in Pittsburgh, God knew what lay ahead for the Church and for our country. God knew the circumstances that awaited us—that is, all of God's people. He knew what we would need, and with extraordinary generosity he awakened those spiritual gifts because we asked him to, and he allowed us to experience his presence with us through the baptism in the Holy Spirit. He taught us and equipped us precisely for this time. But many of us were shortsighted, and after a period of enthusiasm, some of us allowed those gifts to languish. Some among us, in our pews every Sunday, were never sufficiently catechized, and thus never experienced the gifts that lie dormant within us! We failed to be true disciples, to drink from the life-giving streams that are Christ, our Source.

What are we to do? In this book I wish especially to address those who were baptized in the Spirit through the Catholic Charismatic Renewal. I want to provide a handbook of essentials in how to live the Christian life with power, love, and hope—even in the drastic circumstances occasioned by the loss of faith of so many Catholics and among all Christian denominations. How do we have "more" of the Holy Spirit in our lives—his gifts, his fervor, his zeal for souls? How do we become true disciples, willing to do whatever it takes to serve the Lord, using the gifts he has given us?

This is the call to us, brothers and sisters, to you and to me! We can activate the gifts we received in Baptism and Confirmation, the gifts that give us the power of the Holy Spirit to seek the lost and to change lives. We can keep the fire of the Spirit burning, with zeal and fervor, in our hearts. But first, in order to accomplish all that, we have to get back to essentials: daily prayer, Scripture, and the sacraments. In short, we have to become more fully *disciples*. In a very secular society that is often indifferent or even antithetical to the teaching of the gospel, those of us who have experienced the baptism in the Holy Spirit need to be docile, reenergized, and refreshed for the changes ahead. Here's how we can respond to God's initiative, to God's lavish grace.

CHAPTER ONE

Come, Holy Spirit!

I n 1960, Pope John XXIII announced the upcoming Second Vatican Council and asked all Catholics all over the world to pray this prayer:

> Renew your wonders in this our day, as by a new Pentecost. Grant to your Church that, being of one mind and steadfast in prayer with Mary, the Mother of Jesus, and following the lead of blessed Peter, it may advance the reign of our Divine Savior, the reign of truth and justice, the reign of love and peace. Amen.[1]

We prayed it often in our parishes during the three years of the Council. I don't think we had expectations of something tangible or miraculous happening. But the Lord was clearly aware of his people's need. In 1967, two years after the Council ended, God poured out his Spirit in a sovereign act—as in a new Pentecost—on a group of college students at Duquesne University in Pittsburgh, Pennsylvania.

As the students gathered in the chapel for a weekend retreat, they simply asked God to bring alive those gifts given to them in Baptism and Confirmation. At the time, many people knew little about the documents that had been issued by Vatican II or were, unfortunately, indifferent to the Church's teachings. But these students somehow knew that Pope John XXIII's prayer for a fresh outpouring of the Spirit upon the whole Church was a prayer they wanted to see realized.

After dinner on the first night of that retreat, some returned to the chapel. There they again put their request before God. For the next hour, some fell to their knees before the tabernacle, some prostrated themselves; all were overcome by an almost tangible sense of God's presence. That night a few of them committed their lives to the Lord by the power of the Holy Spirit and have never turned back. Quickly did the work of God's mercy—in the Person of the Holy Spirit—begin to spread among college students, first to Notre Dame, then to Michigan State in East Lansing, then to the University of Michigan in Ann Arbor, and then all over the world, involving literally millions of Catholics!

My Own Story

I, too, experienced the baptism of the Holy Spirit, and my story is similar to many others. I will tell it here, as it shows in many ways the state of the Church at the time as well as the mercy of the Lord in granting this great gift to the Church.

At the conclusion of the Council in 1965, I was twenty-six years old, a recently professed religious sister assigned to teaching in a Catholic diocesan high school. I had undergone what I would now call a fairly rigorous formation in which the emphasis was on the externals. The sisters who trained me were good women who loved God and were glad to serve, and so, at the completion of my formation, I thought I was a woman in love with God who wanted to serve him and his Church. But within two years my "strong" faith was badly shaken. In what seemed like a whirlwind, I heard many religious and priests describing our theology as "badly outdated." There was much we needed to do to get up-to-date, they told us. So I began to take advantage of courses and talks to understand the Council in earnest. The many interpretations of the Council documents and other courses on the themes of Vatican II began to confuse me. Some interpretations were very good, some not, but all, good and bad, were often lumped together under the banner of "the teachings of Vatican II." I hesitated to jump on any bandwagon to promote or teach this or that new interpretation of theology, but I was urged by peers to "get on board." Everything was new and exciting, and we didn't have to live any longer under strictures or rules. We were adults; we could form ourselves—decide for ourselves what to believe and what not to believe.

While the *documents* of Vatican II are inspired and good, a fruit of the Holy Spirit, "an independent spirit," it seemed, had seeped into many of the new theories, new interpretations, and even some of the new pastoral practices in the Catholic Church. (Let me say right here that we were formed in those years—the 1940s to the 1960s—more according to the letter of the law than the genuine spirit of the rule, which made us more susceptible to the need for "fresh air.") In our enthusiasm for the "new," however, we abandoned genuine discernment. We were counseled by many so-called teachers of the documents of Vatican II to question everything, including some doctrines of the Church—for example, is Jesus really God? (an old heresy revisited).

Additionally, we were told that we should question the exercise of authority at every level. Was it needed? Couldn't we govern ourselves? Our own secular culture in the U.S. was promoting the same thing, so the message was almost ubiquitous. Suddenly, it seemed that my whole faith life came into question. I even began to question whether there was a God! If there were no God, then my religious life was a sham. So much of what had seemed so settled and clear in my own formation was now up for grabs. I couldn't find clarity when I sought answers, and within two years I had, for all practical purposes, lost my faith. Now, you could say I was immature, relying too much on what others thought and taught. Perhaps that is true. But whatever the source of the problem, the result was profound confusion and a fairly lengthy period of depression.

God's Mercy Is Everlasting

However, God's mercy is everlasting. On one particular day in 1967, I stood by a convent window staring out on a very bleak landscape. "God," I cried, "if you exist, please do something." I expected no answer. As I said, I honestly had substantial doubts that God even existed. If he did exist, he probably didn't hear me, I thought, or if he did hear me, he didn't care enough to answer my pleas. After all, who was I? My little faith was battered almost out of existence.

I turned from the window, planning to go and correct some English essays from the classes I was teaching, but as I turned and stepped away from the window, I walked into a solid barrier, though my eyes could see nothing. I stepped back, stunned, feeling that I was losing my grip on reality. Again I stepped forward and again I bumped into what seemed like a man's chest, though I saw nothing. Then I heard these words, spoken very softly but clearly: "Don't you know I have been with you all the time?" Quietly, in my heart, I said, "No, I didn't," but in that moment I knew with certainty that God existed, that he knew me and loved me, that he had died to save me, and that he would be with me all the days of my life and for all eternity.

That conviction carried me through three more years of seeking and searching to know the truth for myself. I found out which teachers I could trust and which I couldn't. I read—a lot. And I recommitted myself to God over and over again. I learned that God is a very personal God who knows and loves each one of us whom he created. We are not just one of billions. We, each of us, have a unique and very personal relationship with God the Father, God the Son, and God the Holy Spirit. As Blessed John Paul II said, "We are not the sum of our weaknesses and failures; we are the sum of the Father's love for us and our real capacity to become the image of his Son."[2] I recommend that you repeat this over and over—it is the truth!

Another three years went by, and then one winter day, an elderly sister told me that there was a prayer meeting at the local seminary. Would I be willing to drive her? Thinking that this prayer meeting might be one more "new" thing, I was not eager to go. Not that I was opposed to something new, but in this context, I was gun-shy. However, because of her goodness to me in the past, especially during those difficult years, I told her I would take her.

I was not impressed. Forty or so college professors and staff, priests, and laity had gathered together to pray and to hear a talk on the work of the Holy Spirit. This was just a fad, I concluded. "No thanks!" I muttered under my breath. The next week and the week after, the sister again approached me, asking if I would drive her, and I consented. At the third prayer meeting, I again was a spectator. However, the priest spoke about the Holy Spirit and his work to inspire us, to lead us into all truth. There was real assistance in discerning the truth? There was daily help available? I knew that God knew me personally, but I had thought that any real relationship with God would have to wait until heaven. I began to experience a hunger for God that I had not known before. I leaned in and listened more intently.

On the way home, I talked with my companion about what I had heard. She was such a good sister, one who loved God very much and who kept encouraging me to trust him. The very next morning I awoke with these words on my lips: "I want to give my life to God in a way I have never done before." I didn't see how that was possible. I loved God; I had given him my life under the vows of poverty, chastity, and obedience. How could I give him anything more?

Then I thought of a high school friend who had entered a cloistered community about thirty miles from where I was presently stationed. I called her. Though I couldn't speak directly to her on the phone, I was told to come that day to the monastery at two in the afternoon. But how would I get there? One car for nine sisters made it nearly impossible, especially on a Saturday morning, when my request would not seem essential. Just then the doorbell rang, and a sister from another convent said she just stopped to see if anyone needed a ride. She named her destination; her trip would drive us right past the front of the monastery! I was stunned but quickly got in the car and went the twenty-eight miles to the monastery.

When I was able to speak with my friend through the grille, she got down to business quickly. "What do you want?" she asked me. "To give my life to God in a way I have never done before," I replied. "But I don't know what that means . . . I have given him everything, so I don't know what to do." "So," she said, "just tell God that." Feeling a bit foolish, I prayed, "Lord, I want to give my life to you in a way I never have before. I don't know what that means, but you have my life for whatever you want."

We spent some further time in prayer, and then my driver arrived and I left. The next day was devoted to a rehearsal for the play I was directing at the local Catholic high school. Returning to the convent after rehearsal, I slipped into the chapel, and I remember telling the Lord, "If you heard my prayer yesterday, please do something." It wasn't eloquent, but it was enough. I left the chapel and started up a flight of stairs. On a certain step (one that I could find today if I went to that convent!), I experienced something like a pitcher of water being poured over my head—only instead of water, it was joy! "Lord," I said, "what is this?" "It is my Holy Spirit given to you to lead you safely home to me." In my usual pragmatic way, I thought that this joy would not last. But to those of you reading this book, let me say, unequivocally, that it has never left me! Oh, it ebbs and flows, depending on the circumstances of daily life. But it has never left—not for forty-two years! The river of life flows through me, as it does for all the baptized, and I experience it as joy! It was, in effect, my baptism in the Holy Spirit.

God's Gifts Are for Everyone

I don't know why God chose to reveal himself to me in this way, but I *know* beyond the shadow of a doubt that the Holy Spirit, given to us in Baptism and Confirmation, is real. His gifts, understood and yielded to, can change our lives—radically! God did not leave us orphaned; he assured us that he would send us his Spirit. This is what is promised in Scripture. Listen to what Jesus tells us:

> "If you love me, you will keep my commandments. And I will ask the Father, and he will give you another Counselor, to be with you for ever, even the Spirit of truth, whom the world cannot receive, because it neither sees him nor knows him; you know him, for he dwells with you, and will be in you.
>
> "I will not leave you desolate; I will come to you. Yet a little while, and the world will see me no more, but you will see me; because I live, you will live also. In that day you will know that I am in my Father, and you in me, and I in you. He who has my commandments and keeps them, he it is who loves me; and he who loves me will be loved by my Father, and I will love him and manifest myself to him." (John 14:15-21)

This gift of a deep, abiding personal relationship with God is possible for each of us. The seed is given in Baptism; all the grace to grow in wisdom, age, and grace is bestowed on each of us at our baptism. But we must be willing to cooperate and, once we reach the age of reason, to choose more and more to conform our lives to him. We must be willing to enter into that personal relationship on his terms, not ours. "He who does not take his cross and follow me is not worthy of me" (Matthew 10:38).

The spiritual gifts listed in Isaiah 11:2-3 and 1 Corinthians 12, 13, and 14 are meant to be ours. The gifts spoken of in Isaiah are given to shape us more and more into God's image and likeness. These are gifts in which God literally shares *himself,* gifts that truly make us his sons and daughters—not figuratively, but literally! The gifts Paul describes in 1 Corinthians are given to us to enable us to minister to others in God's name! Thus, we are equipped to fulfill our baptismal commitments.

I believe that what John XXIII prayed for, a new Pentecost, this merciful outpouring of his Spirit that so many of us have experienced since 1967, is real and is meant for us all, each of us according to God's will. Different gifts are given to each for different purposes, but to all of us gifts are given so that we may enter a very real and profound personal relationship in order to be more truly his disciples and reach others with his saving love. We are being equipped to be instruments of God to bring the lost, the despairing, the unbelieving, the poor, the weak, the blind, and the lame back to him!

We did not experience what became known as the Charismatic Renewal to form a new movement in the Church. In this work of God, there is no founder—there are many leaders, but no founder except the Holy Spirit. The Holy Spirit pouring out upon us the love of the Father for the Son and the love of the Son for the Father is meant for all the baptized: "As the Father has loved me, so have I loved you; abide in my love" (John 15:9).

Life in the Holy Spirit is not just for those who wish to be part of a group or movement. Life in the Holy Spirit is meant to be the *heart* of the Church! Others, such as Cardinal Leon Joseph Suenens of Belgium, have expressed this sentiment, and I and countless others concur. As many have said, the Charismatic Renewal will have accomplished its purpose when it is lost in the heart of the Church. "If you love me, you will keep my commandments. And I will ask the Father, and he will give you another Counselor, to be with you for ever, even the Spirit of truth, whom the world cannot receive, because it neither sees him nor knows him; you know him, for he dwells with you, and will be in you" (John 14:15-17). God's word is true, and this word is for you. My life and the lives of millions of others are testimony of the truth of God's word and his promises.

CHAPTER TWO

Where Are We Now?

In 1975 I was invited to attend one of the first international meetings of the Catholic Charismatic Renewal in Rome. It was several days of sheer joy, of seeing people literally from every (or at least most) tribe and tongue and people and nation all rejoicing in the incredible mercy of God through his Holy Spirit. What was God about? What did God want to do by allowing us to experience the gifts and fruits of our Baptism and Confirmation so tangibly, as in that first Pentecost?

I remember two experiences during that time that have been indelibly printed on my mind and may help to answer the questions I have just posed.

The first was when, before Mass during the conference, Pope Paul VI was brought in on the portable ceremonial chair, the *Sedia Gestatória*, and carried down the center aisle of St. Peter's Basilica. The Vatican choir was singing, and we were rejoicing as we caught a glimpse of our Holy Father. That day he seemed somber and burdened, yet as he was brought slowly down that aisle, his expression began to change. In the crowd of about ten thousand, a beautiful hymn began to be sung, consisting of only one word, "Alleluia," because it was a word that could be picked up and understood in all languages. The Vatican choir, which was doing a beautiful job with their own hymn, stopped singing (something I would never have expected). They listened for a very brief moment and then joined in with the congregants, and this hymn, with one word, glorified the Lord as I have never known before or since. The pope began to smile, then to nod and turn around, looking at our faces with what I would call a discerning intensity. When he reached the main altar and ascended the stairs, the chorus swelled even more loudly, although that did not seem possible.

At the end of Mass, the pope gestured to Cardinal Leon Joseph Suenens of Belgium, whom he had named to oversee the Charismatic Renewal around the world, to ascend the steps and stand beside him. Then Pope Paul, in an uncharacteristic gesture, put his arm around Cardinal Suenens and stretched out his other arm as if to embrace all of us. That joy, experienced with the pope globally by the grace of God, was beyond my powers of description. It was a hint of heaven.

Sometime later I learned of a remark Pope Paul VI made in relation to some of the difficulties he had faced post-Vatican II: "Referring to the situation of the Church today, the Holy Father says he has the feeling that 'from some fissure the smoke of Satan has entered the temple of God.'"[1] I believe his hope was renewed that day with representatives of the worldwide Charismatic Renewal. He saw that the Holy Spirit was there as a gift, that trusting in the power of the Holy Spirit would enable us to fight the enemy, and that the fulfillment of the prayer "that they may be one" (John 17:22), by the power of the Holy Spirit, was possible.

Just for That Time?

Where are we now? Was that a gift just for a time? Hardly! But it is easy to think so. People who had attended conferences got tired. Indifference, as well as other challenges and obstacles, caused them to cease coming to events. We are a generation used to something new all the time. We drop one thing to pick up another. Perseverance is not always high on our list—and so we can easily fall into looking at the Charismatic Renewal as some kind of a club in which we may have had membership for a time.

We certainly have not been very successful in passing on to the next generations the gifts that have been given to us. God would have taught us if we had asked, but often we had other things to do and other people to see. Life was *so* busy! Unfortunately, it is common with us humans to not see past the noses on our faces. We do that to our own detriment and, many times, to the detriment of those we love.

We were, in fact, novices at allowing the Spirit to exercise his full right over us; we were not the most docile of followers. We tried and in many ways succeeded, but we also failed. Our vision was too small. In the Catholic Charismatic Renewal, we focused on prayer groups and national conferences and "our" ministries and the development of communities. Again, all those projects were good, very good—and needed—but the main focus moved from loving God for himself to the works as ends in themselves. We became focused on particular people and their astounding gifts. At times, we acted as though we were owners of these gifts of God rather than servants, and God allowed much to atrophy.

It is true that many good—even great—works have been borne from the Charismatic Renewal. But God does not look for works first. God desires a personal relationship with each one of us, and it takes daily time and commitment to respond to that offer of a relationship. Because we have been given free will, God will not force himself upon us or command us.

So Much More

Our Father offers his gifts to us through the Spirit to lead us and to help us bring others to a deep and saving knowledge of him. It is a blessing that many healing and deliverance ministries have set countless people free in this country and in countries around the world. I have been blessed to speak in over thirty-one countries, seeing firsthand the love of God for his people, revealed through preaching and teaching in the power of the Holy Spirit. Through healing and deliverance ministries, many people have had great burdens lifted and have gained new trust in a loving Savior. Inspired gifts of preaching and teaching have moved countless Catholics to fully embrace the call to discipleship.

Still, there is so much more God's Spirit wants to do with us and with those who will follow after us. And yet, what he most wants, and wants first in our hearts, is this: our personal love for him, a genuine and ever-growing and deepening personal relationship. As Blessed John Paul II emphasized over and over again, who you *are* in Christ is far more important than what you *do!* Those of us, especially in the U.S., Canada, and Western Europe, need to pay attention to that wisdom and those priorities if we are to bear fruit for his kingdom! As a very wise priest said to me years ago, "You need to learn to distinguish between the 'good thing' and the 'God thing.'" In other words, just because something is good doesn't automatically mean that we should do it. The enemy is wily, and if he can't get to us through actual sin, he will try to wear us out by having us try to do too many "good" works! The Holy Spirit can and will teach us how to discern real good from apparent good. Pray! Discern! Seek wise counsel!

Even with God's generosity to us through his Spirit, even with the teaching and ministry of some outstanding popes over the last forty years, *still* there are many hundreds of thousands of Catholics who do not really *know* Christ. There are many who have left the Church, disillusioned with the scandals and the lack of pastoral care and dedicated teachers of the truth. It is possible that many are being lost eternally. God does not withhold the gifts and power of his Holy Spirit, but we have to *choose* to do it *his* way. Evangelism cannot be seen primarily as a work. The goal of evangelism is a Person; to present the Person of Jesus Christ in such a way that people are drawn to him, not to us or our gifts, but to him! He is the only one who can save, heal, restore, and make well. He is the only one who can truly win souls for his Father. We are his disciples, his servants, here to do his bidding. That requires faith and humility, a kind of poverty that allows him free exercise over our goals, our plans, our direction. His name is to be exalted, not ours.

In terms of the state of society, where we are now is a far cry from the beginning of the renewal in 1967 at Duquesne University. But the prayer in the hearts of those young people—to allow the gifts of their Baptism and Confirmation to be evident for his glory—must be more and more present in our hearts today! The enemy is alive and well, so to speak, but he will be shut out by a poverty of spirit and humility that says, "I depend on Christ and the merits of his death and resurrection for everything!" Such simplicity leads to a single-hearted focus on seeing the One we love most exalted in the heart of every person we meet and to whom we minister. There is no room for freelancers. There is no room for pride, for self-recognition. There must only be room for Jesus. As Blessed John Henry Newman prayed, "Shine through me and be so in me that every soul I come in contact with may feel thy presence in my soul. Let them look up and see no longer me but only thee, O Lord!"

I don't write these words as an idealist. I write them because I am convinced that they are the only tools that will defeat the enemy's work to destroy us. The Church is in very serious need of committed and *surrendered* souls—humble souls who know where their power and virtue come from. Can you be one of them, by the grace of God?

This is what the work of the Holy Spirit in my soul has shown me. What about you? Whether you have been in the Charismatic Renewal since the beginning or whether you have never attended a prayer meeting or gone through a Life in the Spirit Seminar, the Holy Spirit is at work in the Church today seeking souls who will give everything so that he may be known and loved and followed. "Behold, I stand at the door and knock" (Revelation 3:20). Will you respond? There is a work for every person, whether you are in the prime of life or whether you are presently living in a nursing home. All of us are called to be his disciples until we are called home!

To those of us in the renewal: God intimately shared his life with you and me and asked us to be his disciples. I don't think that's a matter of temporary membership. Were you only attracted by novelty and by miracles, or were you attracted by the infinite love of Jesus Christ? Did you give your life to him? Did he pour out gifts upon you? Those gifts were given for a purpose. The day will come when each of us will have to render an account for what we have done with what we have been given. What will you say?

Do We Have Ears to Hear?

The second unforgettable experience for me at that international conference in Rome happened on the last day. Cardinal Suenens was the main celebrant for the Mass. Again, the basilica was full to capacity. I was in the back of the church, barely able to see the altar, but *I was there*. It was May, and it was very warm.

Before the Mass began, I struck up a brief whispered conversation with an elderly Frenchman standing next to me. My French is minimal, but it was sufficient to exchange our joy at being there and our promise to pray for one another. After the consecration, several people around me fainted from the heat and lack of air; some simply had to leave. After Communion, in that physically oppressive environment, there were several prophecies given. Here is one of them:

Because I love you, I want to show you what I am doing in the world today. I want to prepare you for what is to come. Days of darkness are coming on the world, days of tribulation. . . . Buildings that are now standing will not be standing. Supports that are there for my people now will not be there. I want you to be prepared, my people, to know only me and to cleave to me and to have me in a way deeper than ever before. I will lead you into the desert. . . . I will strip you of everything that you are depending on now, so you depend just on me. A time of darkness is coming on the world, but a time of glory is coming for my church, a time of glory is coming for my people. I will pour out on you all the gifts of my Spirit. I will prepare you for spiritual combat; I will prepare you for a time of evangelism that the world has never seen. . . . And when you have nothing but me, you will have everything: lands, fields, homes, and brothers and sisters and love and joy and peace more than ever before. Be ready, my people, I want to prepare you.[2]

This second prophecy followed immediately:

I speak to you of the dawn of a "new age" for my church. I speak to you of a day that has not been seen before. . . . Prepare yourselves for the action that I begin now, because things that you see around you will change; the combat that you must enter now is different; it is new. You need wisdom from me that you do not yet have.

You need the power of my Holy Spirit in a way that you have not possessed it; you need an understanding of my will and of the ways that I work that you do not yet have. Open your eyes, open your hearts to prepare yourselves for me and for the day that I have now begun. My church will be different; my people will be different; difficulties and trials will come upon you. The comfort that you know now will be far from you, but the comfort that you will have is the comfort of my Holy Spirit. They will send for you, to take your life, but I will support you. Come to me. Band yourselves together, around me. Prepare, for I proclaim a new day, a day of victory and of triumph for your God. Behold, it is begun.[3]

As I heard those prophecies, I recognized a certain authenticity. Yes, they would need to be discerned by those who had the authority to do so, but I knew that God was preparing us; he had given us the gift of his Spirit in such remarkable ways that I knew it could not be just for us, but for his people worldwide. As I pondered these words, there were people on my left from another continent who were very overwhelmed by the heat; because they were distracted, they could not "hear" spiritually. Saying, "We must get out of here. It's too hot; I am going to faint," they excused themselves and pushed through the crowd to get air. I understood. But then I glanced to my right, to that elderly Frenchman who was now down on his knees, weeping. In that moment I realized I was being given the privilege of seeing a personal enactment of the parable of the sower and the seed (see Matthew 13:1-23). Some seed fell on rocky ground, some seed fell among thorns, some seed was carried away by birds, and some seed fell on good soil and bore fruit, thirty, sixty, and a hundredfold.

Those who were or still are part of the Charismatic Renewal, do you remember these words from the high altar in St. Peter's? What have you done with them? What are we called to do with them?

Today our need for the Holy Spirit is far more evident. In Ralph Martin's book *Will Many Be Saved?*, he notes that one large American archdiocese, representative of many in the U.S., recorded steep declines—40 to 50 percent over the ten-year period of 2000–2010—in infant baptisms, adult baptisms, Catholic marriages, and those seeking full communion with the Church.[4] In a new book, Martin writes, "As almost 1700 years of Christendom collapse and a new international pagan culture gains ascendency, even rising to the dictatorship of relativism that Benedict warns us about, the Church in the West is encountering circumstances that are more like those encountered by the early Church than anything we have known in our lifetimes. The recent and consistent papal calls for a new Pentecost are perhaps the deepest need in the Church today."[5]

In 1998, before half a million people involved in the new movements in the Church, Pope John Paul II said this:

> The institutional and charismatic aspects are co-essential as it were to the Church's constitution. They contribute, although differently, to the life, renewal, and sanctification of God's People. It is from this providential rediscovery of the Church's charismatic dimension that, before and after the Council, a remarkable pattern of growth has been established for ecclesial movements and new communities. . . . You, present here, are the tangible proof of this "outpouring" of the Spirit. . . . Today, I would like to cry out to all of you gathered here in St. Peter's Square and to all Christians: Open yourselves docilely to the gifts of the Holy Spirit! Accept gratefully

and obediently the charisms which the Spirit never ceases to bestow on us![6]

In 2008, Pope Benedict, reflecting on the text from the first chapter of the Acts of the Apostles in which Jesus promises his disciples that they will be baptized in the Spirit, said this:

> Today I would like to extend the invitation to all: let us rediscover, dear brothers and sisters, the beauty of being baptized in the Holy Spirit; let us recover awareness of our Baptism and our Confirmation, ever timely sources of grace. Let us ask the Virgin Mary to obtain also today a renewed Pentecost for the Church that will imbue in all, and especially in the young, the joy of living and witnessing to the Gospel.[7]

It is my belief that God is asking us *again*, through the repeated calls of John XXIII, Paul VI, John Paul II, and Benedict XVI, and now Pope Francis, to say yes to the call of discipleship, to renewing our assent to the life of a disciple. In the remainder of this book, I will talk about the "essentials"—what we need in order to live the Christian life with power, love, and hope.

CHAPTER THREE

The Call to Discipleship

God is looking for true disciples: those who seek intimacy with the Lord through thought, word, and action. God is asking those who use the gifts of the Holy Spirit to bring many back to him, to help the lukewarm catch fire, to give the desolate true courage and hope, to lift up the downtrodden with their care, and to set the prisoners free from the bonds that led them into sin.

Do you understand that every baptized and confirmed Catholic is called to discipleship? This is not a new spiritual exercise—this is the call of the gospel. We should have learned it as we prepared for Confirmation. Confirmation is a personal call from God to be equipped to bring his light, his truth, his love, and his mercy into every corner, every back alley, every palace, and every place of power; to friends and family, strangers and enemies alike—everywhere to everyone. But unfortunately, a lot of us shrug it off by saying that such a call is for holy people—and that is not me! In his book *The Way of the Disciple,* Erasmo Leiva-Merikakis says this:

> I believe that the call to discipleship in Christianity is universal and does not pertain to a select few. In other words, I would stress that every scene in the Gospel is about discipleship quite simply because the Gospel as such is *kerygma*—a proclamation of encounter with Christ inviting to faith in him and, consequently, to

discipleship. If we have ears attuned to his voice and hearts willing to learn what his Heart has to teach, in every line of the Gospel we will hear Christ calling us to enter into his intimacy and destiny as disciples.[1]

Yes, there is a crucial need for the service of true disciples, but first God wants *each* of us to have a personal relationship with him. Frankly, that's the only way discipleship will bear everlasting fruit. He wants us to live out the baptismal graces and the gifts flowing from Confirmation so that we might mature as his sons and daughters. We are called to begin living part of our inheritance on this earth so that our light might "shine before men, that they may see [our] good works and give glory to [our] Father who is in heaven" (Matthew 5:16).

However, it seems that many of us do not really know who we are in Christ. We do not know what it means to be a son or daughter of God in our everyday life. As a result, we are not able to battle successfully the lethal forces of a secularized culture. Even in the Church, as the people of God, we are disoriented, confused, and, at worst, unwilling and unable to combat the attacks leveled against Christianity. So what are we to do?

We first need to drink from the streams of life-giving water that flow from the side of Christ. We are too easily satisfied with a sip here, a small glass there, that is, a talk, a conference, a retreat, a book that inspires, some time before the Blessed Sacrament. It may seem to satisfy for a brief time, but then we find ourselves parched and needing something colder and more thirst quenching. So unfortunately, instead of turning back to God and spending time with him in prayer, we turn to human answers to quench our thirst, which is really our loneliness. The deepest loneliness in all of us is a loneliness for God, whether we recognize it or not. We were created by God, and we are only complete in him! Loneliness can only be taken away by God as he becomes the center of our lives more and more. Good friends and spouses can help and encourage and love us in a way that assuages our loneliness, but they cannot eradicate it. It is put there by God to remind us that we are never fully whole, never complete, apart from him!

Drinking from Polluted Streams

Part of the source of the severe loneliness and depression encountered by so many in our society is our modern culture, which prizes speed and fast results. In a culture in which fast food, ATM machines, cell phones, and the Internet give us what we want so quickly and are so easily accessible, we begin to see life through those lenses, so to speak. We begin to think that God himself should be more accessible to our needs and desires. So when we turn to God in our need, we are wired to expect an immediate answer. If we don't get it, we conclude either that he isn't there or that he doesn't care. If God really exists and cares about me, we think, then I should be able to quickly—if not immediately—access whatever I need. And when such an immediate answer doesn't occur, we often make the mistake of turning away completely from the only One who can save us, or we may just put him in second place.

Then, experiencing a vacuum mentally, physically, and emotionally, we go out into the highways and byways, drinking from every possible source to try and satisfy the insatiable longings inside us. Money, sex, and power; prestige and influence; control over people and possessions; physical beauty and strength; athletic prowess; popularity of any kind—these are the streams we drink from, and they inevitably fail us. In our confusion and need, we can even resort to alcohol, drugs, and pornography—anything to take away the gnawing hunger and restlessness inside us.

None of those will ever lead us to happiness; none of those things are worthy means or goals for our lives. Only when we put what is first in God's heart first in our own hearts will we ever be satisfied and fulfill the purpose for which we were created. At the very best, the things I have listed here will only give a very temporary reprieve from our loneliness and our need to be loved. Some of our attempts to assuage the pain and loneliness are like dirty water: they will, in the long run, infect us and often can bring death. "You have made us for yourself, O Lord, and our hearts are restless until they rest in you." So wrote St. Augustine, who had drunk from many streams before finding the true wisdom he so abundantly shared in his *Confessions*.

If we find ourselves in this position or in a similar one, then most likely we have been trying to fill the emptiness inside us apart from God. We need to stop! We need to tell God we are sorry for drinking from polluted waters. We need to repent—that is, we need to chart a new course. Repentance is really a change of direction. We stop the direction we have been going and we say to God, "You alone are my Savior, not other people or places or things. I want to choose you as my Savior and to follow the path you have marked out for me." The Scriptures are clear: we have one Savior, our Lord Jesus Christ. Out of love for us, our Father in heaven gave us his Son to lead us safely home, and he gave us his Spirit to gift and equip us as sons and daughters to be followers of his Son, each of us helping one another to return to the Father, where there will be no more mourning or weeping or pain or death (Revelation 21:4). That's God's promise, and God does not lie!

A Change in Direction

But because we are imperfect, we often forget who we are and where we are going. We are made for God—for union with the source of all love, beauty, truth, and goodness, but we can get distracted or sidetracked and ultimately diverted into drinking deeply from polluted streams. Thus, we become separated from the only Source that gives true life! When we don't have our direction set clearly, we can end up drinking from man-made streams that never satisfy—whether it be what the world offers, what the flesh craves, or what Satan masterminds to thwart us from our true purpose and end.

Yes, there really is a Satan, a fallen angel who, out of pride, rejected God and placed himself as the center of *his* "kingdom." I know it can sound like a fairy tale, but it is real. Read Genesis. Read about the temptation of Jesus in the Gospel of Matthew (4:1-11). If Jesus himself was tempted, why do we think we should be exempt? We often exclude the work of evil as a source of many of our difficulties, but to exclude Satan as a source of some of our problems is to be blind. On the other hand, to blame him for everything is just as bad. There is personal responsibility, and we need to take responsibility for what we can change.

But there is an enemy, the enemy of our souls, and we need to learn how to discern his activity in our lives; we need to understand our vulnerabilities to the attacks of the devil so that we can defeat his influence in our lives. God has power over all evil. If we reject the enemy's enticements and his subtle lies, if we quickly repent when we have succumbed and bring the battle to the Lord in prayer for help, God will bless and restore and heal. *Again, we need to bring our battles to him for his saving help!* That's the key to victory: bring the battle to the Lord. Don't try to defeat the temptations on your own. Take them to Jesus. Ask him to teach you how to fight and win.

So how do we go about accepting our call to discipleship? What does that mean? You might be saying or thinking these sorts of things: "I've followed the Lord for many years; I think I am a faithful Catholic, but I feel somewhat clueless and helpless in dealing with the current issues." "Can anything be done, or do we just have to endure?" "I'm tired of all the fighting— I just want peace!" "Who can you trust, anyway? I don't trust most politicians, and I certainly don't trust most priests, given the sex abuse scandal in the Church." All of these kinds of negative and defeatist attitudes lead to widespread discouragement among many Christians, and certainly among Catholics in particular. What are we to do?

The Path of Daily Prayer

[Jesus] went up on the mountain, and called to him those whom he desired; and they came to him. And he appointed twelve, to be with him, and to be sent out to preach and have authority to cast out demons. (Mark 3:13-15)

This passage in Mark's Gospel, when Jesus is calling his apostles, is one of the simplest and yet most profound set of verses in the entire Gospel, and it can be applied to us, his disciples, as well. It has a very substantial lesson for us.

"A great multitude" of people from Galilee, Judea, Jerusalem, Idumea, Tyre, and Sidon were surrounding Jesus and seeking healing (Mark 3:7, 8). Jesus had already healed many and cast out demons, but the enormous crowd continued to besiege him. Jesus even feared being crushed by the crowds, all of whom sought to touch him (3:9-10). Here he was in the midst of great and very obvious need. What did Jesus do? At a certain point, he withdrew from the crowd and began to climb into the hills (3:13)! Jesus always went up to the hills or the mountains when he needed a particular time for prayer, time to commune with his heavenly Father. Right there, in that action, we see something most essential for a disciple: the willingness to put his relationship with his Father first! If Jesus did it, we need to do likewise.

Even in the midst of the people's great physical and spiritual needs, Jesus withdrew to the mountain to spend time with his Father—to spend time in prayer. We can do no less. It has to be our priority each day. It may vary in length according to our state in life and our responsibilities, but there is no way we can be true and active disciples of Christ without first spending time in daily prayer, daily time alone with the Lord. These first disciples did not make excuses about needing to minister to the crowds; they followed Jesus, and his first priority was to spend time with his Father—again, let me emphasize—even in the midst of obvious need. They followed him up the mountain and made themselves available to him. They heard his voice.

Have you learned how to still your heart so that you can hear Jesus and do his bidding when he calls you? A relationship with the Father comes before all service, and no relationship can grow without some time daily with him! This is the only path to learning to know the Father, the only path to true discipleship. Jesus will teach us and lead us to the Father; he will teach us how to hear the Father's voice and obey. "I do as the Father has commanded me, so that the world may know that I love the Father" (John 14:31). Do you hear his voice? A personal, daily relationship with God is essential for a disciple, and God wants to give it to us; he wants to share with us his life with the Father, even more than we want to receive it. In this personal relationship lies the answer to our loneliness, our fear, our anger, our confusion, our profound discouragement, and, at times, even our despair.

Why is all this possible? Because you truly are a son or daughter of God, and God desires that you share even now in the first pledge of your inheritance: the Holy Spirit.

So then, brethren, we are debtors, not to the flesh, to live according to the flesh—for if you live according to the flesh you will die, but if by the Spirit you put to death the deeds of the body you will live. For all who are led by the Spirit of God are sons of God. For you did not receive the spirit of slavery to fall back into fear, but you have received the spirit of sonship. When we cry, "Abba! Father!" it is the Spirit himself bearing witness with our spirit that we are children of God, and if children, then heirs, heirs of God and fellow heirs with Christ, provided we suffer with him in order that we may also be glorified with him. (Romans 8:12-17)

Examining Our Hearts

So, in what I believe is a strong call to discipleship, we need to ask ourselves a question: Is our faith in God the bedrock of our lives, or is it just one aspect of what we call our life? Sr. Ruth Burrows, an outstanding spiritual writer, "hits the nail on the head" about living the life of faith. I will quote her extensively because I want you to be challenged, as I was.

Faith is not a thing of the mind; it is not an intellectual certainty or a felt conviction of the heart. *It is a sustained decision to take God with utter seriousness as the God of my life.* It is to live out each hour in a practical, concrete affirmation that God is Father and that he is "in heaven." It is a decision to shift the centre of our lives from ourselves to him, to forego self-interest and make his interests, his will our sole concern.[2] (Emphasis mine)

Each of us has the choice either to live by faith or to live by "flesh." To live by "flesh" is to live within the limits of our own potential, within the limits of our own perception and understanding, according to how things seem and feel, according to our natural *experience*. It is instinctive for us to live thus, taking for granted that our conscious experience is to be trusted, that it is the way things really are, the way we are, the way God is—that this *is* our life. We want to remain on this level because it is within our grasp; it is "ours" and affords a sort of security and assurance. This is so natural to us . . . that we are unaware of how much of our life is lived from self, relying on self and not on faith in the Son of Man. We cannot rid ourselves of this deeply rooted pride and self-possession by our own strength. Only the Holy Spirit of the Crucified and Risen One can effect it, and this he is indeed always trying to do. But we must recognize his work, and respond "Amen."[3]

To say, "Amen" is to say, "So be it. May my life be lived in faith of your creation, of my purpose, and of my eternal destiny. So be it, Lord. I will follow you." Can you say those words? If we are earthly bound, we cannot let go of our attachments to the things of this earth. It takes grace flowing from the gift of faith to see ourselves as we truly are: weak, sinful creatures in need of a Savior. But when we admit our poverty—"I am not the source of my own life, I cannot save myself for eternal life, I need a Savior"—then we are on the path to true faith.

Obedience to the Lord, to his word, and to his teaching through our popes and bishops is a sure protection from the worst onslaughts of the enemy, who wants to take us away from the truth. He wants to sever our relationship from the One who said, "I am the way, and the truth, and the life" (John 14:6). Truth, you see, is a Person. Satan hates him and will do all he can to dissuade us from following him!

Post-Vatican II brought a breath of fresh air; the work of the Holy Spirit did happen. But under our radar, so to speak, came another wind, the wind of change for change's sake, a wind that sowed confusion and uncertainty and, in some cases, outright rebellion. The Holy Spirit was given to us, in part, to give us a spirit of discernment so that we would know how to distinguish the false from the good. It takes humility to receive that gift and use it in the power of the Holy Spirit.

The Holy Spirit is the love between the Father and the Son—a love so great, so infinite, that it "generates" the third Person of the Blessed Trinity. When we are obedient to the Lord, to his word, to the teachings of the Church—in short, to the truth—we can be eventually brought into union with Love itself!

Let me speak now to those of you who were or are part of the Charismatic Renewal. If you would, please spend a few moments reflecting on these questions.

- Did you first participate in the Charismatic Renewal because it sounded good and exciting and new? When it no longer excited you, did you get bored and walk away? Was it only a kind of novelty?

■ Did you come only to assuage your own hurts? Were you only looking for your own relief? Did you sense that God had more for his people?

■ Did you see yourself as a steward and servant of God's gifts to be used for his glory, or were they only for your personal fulfillment?

■ When there was a price, did you withdraw your time, your talents, or your gifts? Did you see yourself as the owner of those gifts who could decide when and where and under what conditions you would use them? Do you know what it means to be a servant of the gifts of God?

We must recognize the gift of the Holy Spirit as a true gift, one to be nourished and celebrated in a personal relationship with God, a relationship that will enable us to work with God to bring many back from the point of hell. God wants us to stand firm over the years and be faithful to him and to his people, putting our gifts at his service so that we are wealthy, not in the world's eyes, but in God's. God wants us to sacrifice our time and talents in order that we can use the gifts he has bestowed on us. We are meant to be like servants and handmaids with our lamps trimmed, ready at the Lord's beckoning. We are truly meant to be light radiating from Christ, shining through us to bring many to himself. We are the stars that will shine for all eternity.

This was God's plan when you received the baptism in the Holy Spirit. Have you cooperated with God's plan?

As you reflect on these questions, you may need to repent of taking God's precious gifts too lightly. It is essential that we give to God an account of our stewardship of the graces he has bestowed. What have we done with them? Have we invested them, using them with gratitude and love? Have the effects of those gifts been multiplied for his glory? "Every one to whom much is given, of him will much be required" (Luke 12:48). We are called by God through our Baptism and Confirmation to be his disciples, men and women who live for the life that awaits us in heaven with God.

Into what general category do you fall? Do you understand that God offers his invitation of a deep and personal relationship with him no matter what our present circumstances are and no matter what motives may have brought each of us into the Charismatic Renewal in the first place?

Your honest answers to these questions may mean the difference between heaven and hell for those you relate to, work with, and encounter day in and day out. God's intention is to use each of us to reach others, to help lead people into the very heart of God. Your life deeply affects the lives of others, for good or for ill, whether you are aware of it or not.

Are You Willing?

To those of you who have never participated in the Catholic Charismatic Renewal, this book can help you too. Why? Because every one of us is invited, especially by the graces of Baptism and Confirmation, to enter into a profound and intensely personal relationship with God. The deepest desires of each person's heart, whatever they may be, can only be fully satisfied in accepting Christ's invitation to "follow me." The Holy Spirit's presence in our soul through Baptism and Confirmation is not a symbol! God dwells within us by his Spirit in order to lead us into the fullness of truth, beauty, and goodness. He is *absolute truth, absolute beauty,* and *absolute goodness,* and it is in union with God that we find our fulfillment and destiny.

Let's look again at the fundamentals. God calls us—each individual Christian—into a personal, intimate relationship with him. But that involves surrender on our part. God wants to occupy the center of our lives. Stubborn and proud as we are, we seek a compromise. "Let's lead my life together, Lord." But it doesn't work that way *if you want to be a disciple!* There is a certain sense in which we need to give up control and allow him to exercise full authority. That essentially is what happens in the baptism in the Holy Spirit; it's an adult, personal decision to put him dead center in our lives and then accept the gifts he gives through Baptism and Confirmation in order to serve his people. "Do you not know that your body is a temple of the Holy Spirit within you, which you have from God? You are not your own; you were bought with a price. So glorify God in your body" (1 Corinthians 6:19-20).

You and I have been called by the last several popes to pray for a new Pentecost in our time. Popes Paul VI, John Paul II, Benedict XVI, and Francis have called us to a New Evangelization, and just as it was with the early disciples, there cannot be a New Evangelization without a new Pentecost. For what, then, do we pray? How do we proceed from this point on? *Desire, more than anything else in life, to do the will of God. Seek deeper conversion!* This is the heart of discipleship!

The Holy Spirit is waiting for us to say YES again. He wants us sober, committed, and ready to do whatever the Father asks. Your decision will make all the difference for you, yes, but also for countless others who still wander in the darkness with little or no faith.

CHAPTER FOUR

Keep the Fire Burning

How do we accept the call to discipleship with eagerness, enthusiasm, and fervor, willing to lay our lives down for the Lord, no matter the cost? How do we keep the fire of the Holy Spirit burning in our hearts? In this chapter, I will deal with some absolute essentials in the life of a disciple: prayer, Scripture, the Eucharist, and study. I will also mention some potential obstacles that can keep us from deepening our relationship with the Lord.

As I have stressed in the preceding chapters, spending quiet time with the Lord each day is crucial. You can pray in many ways, including just spending time at the foot of the Lord in silence. To live the life of a disciple, you need to find time daily for God—and you can if you really want to. As I have said in talks around the world, you wouldn't say, "I don't have time to go to the bathroom." You can't; you must go! Look at a daily time with the Lord in the same way—it is just as urgent spiritually! (Pardon the crudity, but I want you to understand how imperative it is.) As St. Augustine wrote, we must never tire of praying:

> Many people grow weary of prayer. In their first prayer after conversion they pray ardently, then later more lazily, then rather coldly, and at last quite negligently: they think themselves secure. The enemy is on the watch, and you are asleep. But the Lord commanded in the

gospel that we must pray always, and not give up (Luke 18:1). . . . We must not grow weary, then, in our prayer. God may delay, but he will not disappoint us over what he means to grant. Fully confident in his promise, we must not get tired of praying; and if we persevere, this, too, is by his good gift.[1]

Feed on Scripture

If we want our faith to grow, we have to feed it food that comes from God. Often we have our hearts and minds and spirits set on food that destroys, or we have the right food but we try to live on what would be classified as a starvation diet. To grow healthy in your spiritual life, please take time each day to read Scripture. God's word has the power to literally change your life. His word is "living and active, sharper than any two-edged sword" (Hebrews 4:12). So read it daily! It will change your thinking and your priorities; it will build your faith and empower and strengthen you. As God's Spirit acts in your life, you will be more able to discern and respond. Without God's word, we can easily be deaf, dumb, and blind to God's action. Its power doesn't come primarily through our senses but through God's action in our soul! When you begin to choose to desire God's will, you will see the fruit of God-given desires.

Fr. George Montague, a noted Scripture scholar, said years ago, "If you want to *understand* the word of God, *stand under* it!" In other words, don't judge it; let it judge you. Put yourself under its authority daily. This is very sound advice; this is the discipline that helps to shape a true disciple.

There are many plans for reading Scripture that can be fruitful. One plan is to take the readings of the day at Mass, pray them quietly to yourself, and then apply them to your daily life. In my weekday radio program *Food for the Journey*, I try to show how God's word can feed us, nourish us, and give us hope in our daily circumstances. It is aired on more than one hundred Catholic stations in the U.S. If you don't have access to Catholic radio, or if the timing of the program does not fit into your schedule, go to the radio page of our Renewal Ministries website, and listen to it. You can also download it on your iPod or phone and can listen to it at your convenience.

Feed on the Eucharist

Another important way to nourish your relationship with Jesus is to feed on the Eucharist as often as you can. Whenever it is possible, even if it is inconvenient, go to daily Mass. Receive nourishment from the word and the Bread of Life. Here is the fountain of life: drink deeply. If you can't make it to daily Mass, either because no Mass is available or because of health reasons or serious commitments to job or family, then take a few minutes each day to read the daily Mass readings, asking God for the grace to apply them to your life that day. Then make a spiritual communion like this one, which was recommended by St. Alphonsus Liguori:

> My Jesus, I believe that you are present in the most Blessed Sacrament. I love you above all things, and I desire to receive you into my soul. Since I cannot now

receive you sacramentally, come at least spiritually into my heart. I embrace you as if you have already come and unite myself entirely to you. Never permit me to be separated from you. Amen.

Here is another prayer of spiritual communion, composed by Cardinal Rafael Merry del Val:

At your feet, O my Jesus, I prostrate myself, and I offer you repentance of my contrite heart, which is humbled in its nothingness and in your holy presence. I adore you in the Sacrament of your love, the ineffable Eucharist. I desire to receive you into the poor dwelling that my heart offers you. While waiting for the happiness of sacramental communion, I wish to possess you in spirit. Come to me, O my Jesus, since I, for my part, am coming to you! May your love embrace my whole being in life and in death. I believe in you, I hope in you, I love you. Amen.

Eucharistic Adoration

If there is Eucharistic adoration in your parish or at a parish close by, whether daily, weekly, or monthly, take advantage of it. It is a time of adoration and thanksgiving before your Eucharistic Lord. Choose psalms of thanksgiving and praise. Read them in his presence, making them your own. Blessed Pope John Paul II gave us some wonderful help in *Novo Millennio Ineunte*. In this apostolic letter, he calls us into a time of adoration by urging us to ponder and meditate on the suffering face of Christ.[2] To do that, I recommend praying with chapters 52 and 53 of the Book of Isaiah, which are known as the "Suffering Servant" passages. Read these verses slowly, stopping when something strikes you. Let what God did for you penetrate to the marrow of your bones—and it can, through the grace of the Holy Spirit and his action in your life!

Pope John Paul II also urged us to meditate on the risen face of Christ. We can do that by reading and reflecting on the Gospel passages that speak of the resurrection and Jesus' appearances to his disciples. As you persevere in this practice recommended by John Paul, I think you will find that the depth of your understanding of what Jesus has done on your behalf and what awaits you when you meet him face-to-face will grow. As you continue in this devotional practice, many graces will come to you! One warning: don't get discouraged. I pray this way often, and I am tired and distracted a lot of the time. But I have persevered, and many graces have become quietly evident in my own life over time. Remember, God is not an ATM machine; he does not operate on our schedule.

In a later section of this same letter, *Novo Millennio Ineunte,* Pope John Paul elaborates on personal prayer:

> It [the mystical tradition of the Church] shows how prayer can progress, as a genuine dialogue of love, to the point of rendering the person wholly possessed by the divine Beloved, vibrating at the Spirit's touch, resting filially within the Father's heart. This is the lived experience of Christ's promise: "He who loves me will

be loved by my Father, and I will love him and manifest myself to him" (John 14:21). It is a journey totally sustained by grace, which nonetheless demands an intense spiritual commitment and is no stranger to painful purifications (the "dark night"). . . . Yes, dear brothers and sisters, our Christian communities must become *genuine "schools" of prayer,* where the meeting with Christ is expressed not just in imploring help but also in thanksgiving, praise, adoration, contemplation, listening and ardent devotion, until the heart truly "falls in love."[2]

Intercession

Another part of daily, or at least weekly, prayer should be intercession for your needs and those of your family and friends. This is an area where Satan can ply his "tools" to discourage us so much that we stop interceding. Never, never! So often we wring our hands and are even sometimes oppressed when crosses come to us in life. Believe me, I understand. Some things come without warning, and they can knock us down. Bring all your needs to God—all of them, great and small. Jesus tells us that whatever we ask for in his name will be granted.

Make sure that, as Scripture exhorts us, you are offering your prayers and petitions in *his* name—not in your name, but in his. We have received a great promise: "If you ask anything of the Father, he will give it to you in my name" (John 16:23). What does it mean to ask in Jesus' name? It doesn't mean just saying Jesus' name at the end of your prayer, although that can be a sign of our faith in God. But you cannot just pay lip service. Saying the word, the name, is not enough.

When I was a young teenager, my father, a mechanic, would send me to the auto parts store in the little town where we lived. Small-town living meant that almost everyone knew everyone else. So I would go to the store and tell the owners that my dad wanted these parts for the cars he was repairing and that he would pay them at the end of the week. No one questioned me; they knew my father well. I used my father's name to get these materials, and because they trusted my father, they gave them to me. They knew I was asking for what my father wanted! (I always liked looking at the seat covers and floor mats, but I think if I had tried to include those in my purchases, the owners might have legitimately wondered if my father had really asked for them.)

When we ask in Jesus' name, we first have to ask ourselves if this is what Jesus really wants us to have. I cannot ask in his name without knowing his will, just as I could not ask for something in my earthly father's name if my father had not given me permission to do so. What God wants most for each of us is that we know his love and respond to it by following him more closely. When we are praying for something good for someone we love, our vision is often shortsighted. We can see a good, and so we ask for that—perhaps something regarding finances, health, or relationships. But is that what the Father wants for our loved one at that time? Meanwhile, God knows the state of the soul of the one for whom we pray, and he may know that there is a more important gift that he wishes to give. If the person were to receive what we were praying for, he or she might just be satisfied and not look further, especially when it comes to questions of salvation. So we want to ask in Jesus' name!

Let me share an example with you. A young woman came to me in tears because she and her boyfriend had just broken up, and she was devastated. She loved him and thought that marriage was in the offing. I told her that God loved her even more and that he had a plan for her life that was good. I prayed that she could trust God, but I never prayed that she and her boyfriend would be reconciled. It seemed that every time I tried to pray that way, something stopped me. So I asked the Lord, "What do you want me to pray for?" And I sensed (with no audible words) that I should pray that she would give her whole heart to God and put him at the center of her life. I prayed the way I thought God was asking me, and two years later it bore tremendous fruit in a marriage with another young man who had God at the center of his life. The Holy Spirit will teach you how to pray for yourself and for others. Intercessory prayer is one of the greatest acts of mercy we can perform for those we love and for those who ask for our help.

One of the greatest saints committed to intercessory prayer was St. Monica. She prayed for many years for the conversion of her son, St. Augustine. Nothing seemed to change. In fact, things got worse! At one point, she especially prayed that God would not allow her son to go to Rome. It was so pagan that her son would never stand a chance of becoming a Christian, she understandably thought. Yet when Augustine did go to Rome, Monica did not despair but trusted God to hear her long-suffering prayer for her wayward son. From Rome Augustine went to Milan, where he met the bishop, St. Ambrose, who eventually baptized Augustine into life in Christ. Never give up! Never stop praying.

Have the courage to pray this way for your spouse, your children, your grandchildren, and your friends. Sometimes we just want the difficulty solved; we don't want to live through the anguish or pain of watching people we love suffer. It may take longer to see the fruit in the lives of our loved ones if we pray according to God's will—longer, that is, than we want to wait—but the fruit can be eternal. Put first in your heart and prayer what is first in God's heart and prayer. Read Matthew 6:25-33; seek first the kingdom of God in your intercession for others, and you will see blessings. Pray like this: "Thy kingdom come, thy will be done in the lives of all those I love." This is the way the Holy Spirit works, and it can make your prayer very fruitful. We are very shortsighted in eternal matters! "Help me, Lord, to see things from your perspective."

Study

As part of prayer, at least weekly, spend some time reading books that will help you to grow spiritually. Turn off the TV, the computer, the iPod, and the CD player. There are many good books that can help you grow. Five among them that I especially recommend are as follows: *Bible Basics for Catholics* by Dr. John Bergsma; *Essence of Prayer* by Sr. Ruth Burrows, OCD; *The Gift of Faith* by Fr. Tadeusz Dajczer; *The Way of the Disciple* by Erasmo Leiva-Merikakis; and *The Fulfillment of All Desire* by Ralph Martin. Read them slowly! Let the truths take root in your heart. I would also recommend reading good biographies of the saints. Purchase or rent some good DVDs on the lives of saints. Watching one of those films gets my life back in focus.

We are pulled hither and yon by so many things every day. We are bombarded by "noises" of all kinds. At best, this wearies and distracts us. The Holy Spirit is truly speaking to our hearts and spirits a great deal, but if we are surrounded by so many other voices, how do we think we can hear that "still, small voice," that fatherly voice of love, wisdom, correction, and hope? I offer these suggestions as a practical way of protecting your mind and heart, of making it more of a home for the Holy Spirit.

Possible Roadblocks

Our prayer, Scripture reading, study, and participation in the sacraments, especially the Eucharist, will give us the power we need to answer God's call to discipleship. However, we must be aware that this power can be blocked by our attitudes. According to St. Thomas Aquinas, we may fail to fully live the Christian life when we allow the following attitudes to take root in our hearts:

Lack of Faith. Simply reciting the Creed every Sunday and believing it *are not enough for faith to grow*. It has to become a conviction of the mind and the heart! Pope Benedict put it this way:

Faith is an orientation of our existence as a whole. It is a fundamental option that affects every domain of our existence. Nor can it be realized unless all the energies of our existence go into maintaining it. Faith is not merely intellectual, or merely volitional, or merely emotional activity—it is all of these things together. It is an act of the whole self, of the whole person. . . . Faith is a perishing of the mere self and precisely thus a resurrection of the true self. To believe is to become oneself through liberation from the mere self, a liberation that brings us into communion with God mediated by communion with Christ.[4]

In a similar way, Sr. Ruth Burrows talks about what is necessary to truly believe:

Deep within every human heart—unless it has been profoundly purified—there lurks a sly, unrecognized cunning, all too well skilled in self-deception and evasion. This is the total adversary of belief. It is the cunning of pride, of self-possession, of self-sufficiency. To live fully out of our inheritance, to live solely by the faith of the Son of God, to live the life of Jesus—all this may sound beautiful (and beautiful it indeed is, beyond our wildest dreams), but in practice it strikes a deadly blow at human pride. This is why so many, face to face *in reality* with the self-dispossession that life in Jesus calls for, walk no more with him—not in the sense of complete desertion and denial of belief, but rather because they have said "No" to *his* cross, however many other crosses they may be carrying supposedly in his name.[5]

This is another section of Sr. Ruth's book that is too long to just summarize. I want you to read it and, hopefully, reread it. It provides a profound examination of conscience on the root causes of a lack of faith. May such an examination lead to repentance for you, as it has done for me!

Lack of Authentic Repentance. Am I genuinely sorry for my sins? Do I reflect on the pain I cause the One who loves me infinitely more than anyone ever could in this world? Do I understand that conversion is a sign of genuine repentance and needs to be a part of daily life?

Let me give you an example. Many years ago, Fr. Michael Scanlan, TOR, former president of Franciscan University of Steubenville, told some students this story. When he was a very young man, he spent a season in the merchant marines. One of his main jobs was the 4:00 a.m. watch as the ship brought fruit and other goods from Hawaii to New York via the Panama Canal.

Every day at 4:00 a.m., young Michael was on deck, and one day he asked the navigator why he had to check the coordinates so often. "If you've set the wheel with appropriate coordinates and then locked it in place, and I am here on watch, why do you keep checking the wheel every so many hours?" The navigator responded, "Because of the wind, the waves, the storms, the water temperature—all can throw a ship off course. If we were off by even a degree or less, we could end up in Argentina instead of going through the Panama Canal!"

Fr. Michael told the students that this was the best analogy he knew of to show why we need ongoing conversion. The winds of daily life, the temperature of daily interaction, and the storms of life can easily throw us off course. Repentance and conversion are the ways to reset, to adjust the wheel to make sure we are on course for heaven. I heard that homily maybe thirty-two years ago, and it has guided my life ever since.

Daily, take a few moments and ask the Lord, "How have I served you today?" Ask the Lord to show you where you have failed, and then repent. Then ask him where you have succeeded, and give him praise and thanksgiving. Once you have received God's forgiveness, reset your personal goals for the next day. You will be amazed at the clarity and growing peace and confidence that God will give you through his Spirit. You are giving the Spirit room to direct your daily life!

Lack of Understanding. Do you truly understand who God is, who you are, and where you are going? Take time at least once a week to sit quietly and acknowledge (even out loud) who you are: a son or daughter of the living God. You have a Father in heaven who loves you and who seeks to lead you closer and closer to himself. Your sonship or daughterhood is your most significant and foundational identity. The world will tell you that if you do not have the latest in everything, if you are not beautiful or handsome, if your bank account isn't growing, if you do not share its definition of popularity or influence, then you are worth nothing. *None of these things or others like them will last.* What *will last* is who you are and to whom you belong.

Ask the Holy Spirit for the grace to believe that the gifts of faith, hope, and love in God and for God are the true priceless treasures. God will give you eternal riches and a place in his kingdom forever. That is not a fairy tale; it's real. Do you understand who you are by Baptism? Do you believe that you have an eternal destiny where every tear will be wiped away?

Lack of Desire. Lack of intention and desire to live a new way of life as a Christian disciple can block the fruitfulness of the sacraments and of the baptism in the Holy Spirit, which is the conscious, mature desire to activate all the gifts received in the sacraments. God will never force himself or intrude in our lives. He has given us that marvelous gift of free will. Don't misuse it. Let your will—your choices, your decisions—be under God's authority. Ask for the grace to desire the good in every situation. Through your cooperation with that prayer, you will come to know the source of all life-giving desire: Jesus himself!

Failure to Address Demonic Activity. There really is a heaven; there really is a hell. There really is a God; there really is a fallen angel who is called Satan, and he tries to divert and tempt us from what God wants for us. Chapter 8 of this book, "Put on the Whole Amor of God," which is based on Ephesians 6:10-18, offers guidance on how to combat the enemy.

Of course, we do not want to see Satan behind every trial or frustration or even disaster, but we do want to learn to recognize that he is the father of lies and that he will try to discourage, distract, or even turn us away from the Lord. We want to learn how to detect him and take authority over the power he tries to exert in our lives. That authority is given to us in Baptism.

A lot of damage could be avoided in our personal lives and in our families if we would learn to discern what is truly an evil temptation from what are just our own weaknesses and faults. Ultimately, what God is after in your life is *your willingness to be his disciple.* That is why his Holy Spirit was poured out in the beginning. The first apostles and disciples had heard and accepted Jesus as the promised Messiah. They knew the truth, but in their human nature, they felt helpless to communicate it to others. They were afraid and limited in articulating what Jesus had taught them and what he had shown them about how to live. They had no power to face the formidable structures and authorities of their day. So they waited in that upper room until God chose to visit them.

Disciples are those whose eyes, even in the midst of daily life, are fixed on the prize: life with the Source of all love and goodness and truth, the heaven that awaits us. *We need to adjust our focus and make some personal decisions if we are going to be disciples of Christ!* We need God's love and power, and we can only receive them if we decide to spend time with God.

CHAPTER FIVE

Coming to Know the True God

How do you envision God? As we establish (or reestablish) a regular daily prayer time, we need to honestly look at how we see God—this God to whom we are giving our lives. As we do, we discover the reality of who God is in the Blessed Trinity of three Persons in communion with one another. And that opens the way for the Holy Spirit to bestow on us more gifts, as we continue to yield our lives to his life-giving grace.

Many people today find it difficult to relate to God the Father because they had negative experiences with their own father, or because they never had a relationship with a father at all. And yet God our Father is the source of life for each of us. He seeks to protect, strengthen, and encourage us; he seeks to foster our gifts, our talents, and our abilities. He rejoices to see us grow and reveal him through our thoughts, words, and actions.

This is the role of a father, even on a biological level, and the importance of a father cannot be overstated. "Young men who grow up in homes without fathers are twice as likely to end up in jail as those who come from traditional two-parent families," even when other factors such as race, income, and parent-education levels are held constant.[1] The overwhelming majority of youths who commit suicide, exhibit behavioral disorders, drop out of high school, or are in juvenile detention facilities are from homes without fathers.[2] Some research shows that "boys who grow up in father-absent homes are more likely than those in father-present homes to have trouble establishing appropriate sex roles and gender identity."[3] Many, many children today don't have an earthly father who cares; they don't have a father present to guard, protect, and defend them. No wonder we are in trouble! As Blessed John Paul II said, "As the family goes, so goes the nation, and so goes the whole world in which we live."[4]

Brothers and sisters, God revealed himself to us through Jesus Christ. Jesus revealed to us the Father of us all—the Father who loves us and sent his only Son to die for us so that we could be united one day as the true family of God and so that our lives might bear fruit for all eternity. Christ, by his obedience and love of the Father, made a way for us to live eternally. You have a Father! Whether or not we know our earthly father, whether we believe that we have an eternal Father who wants to care for us now through this life, every day God our Father provides ways to bring us safely through this life and, eventually, home to him.

Even as I write this, I am thinking of the many men in this country who have tried in every way to be good fathers, but circumstances prevented them from carrying out their responsibilities as they would have wished. I have spoken to many of you. You are an absent father without intending to be. Pray for your children. Ask God to do for them what you cannot. Ask God to show you the ways you can be a good father even under trying circumstances. Don't give up; God will hear your prayer!

Single mothers, you carry a heavy burden as well, often greater than the men, but God is all-merciful. No matter what has happened, remember: *you have a Father in heaven* to turn to in your need. Learn to pray daily to your heavenly Father for yourself and for your children. Entrust your children to their

Father in heaven. *Teach them that they have a Father*—a real Father. Teach them how to approach their Father in heaven. The Holy Spirit will inspire you so that your children will trust that they have a Father who cares. *God can do what you cannot.* Trust him!

The Prayer of Jesus

No matter what our situation is, we need to learn to turn to our heavenly Father. He will not be outdone in generosity! Here is one way to grow in your own relationship with God your Father and can help your children to do the same: pray the Lord's Prayer. Don't just say the words—really pray them.

"Our Father . . . "
St. Paul tells us that the Holy Spirit in us cries out, "Abba!"—that is, "Father!" (Romans 8:15; Galatians 4:6). The Holy Spirit, given to you in the sacraments of Baptism and Confirmation, cries out through you to the Father, revealing you to him. The word "Abba" is an Aramaic word that means "Papa," "Daddy," or other such childlike and endearing terms. It is a name filled with affection and trust. It signifies that the Spirit wishes us to claim our baptismal heritage, to enter into a personal relationship with our Father who is in heaven; and the Holy Spirit will reveal him to us if we ask. Remember, Jesus promised us, "Ask, and it will be given you" (Matthew 7:7). Scripture tells us that we do not receive because we do not ask (James 4:2). To "ask" means to come to our heavenly Father with faith, seeking from him what we need. We need to have confidence that, because he

is a good Father, if it is a good thing that we ask for, then it shall be given to us. If it is not a good thing, God will redirect our intention to what is good—if we give him that freedom. He is a Father; he wants to guide, to direct, and to give us the best, but to receive, we need to sit at his feet and let him teach us. Learn at the feet of the Father how to be a true son or daughter. Ask Jesus to teach you. Read the whole Gospel of John. Take time to read a chapter a day, and see how Jesus loves and obeys his Father. We are called and empowered by the Holy Spirit to go and do likewise.

And therein lies our security.

When I was a child of about seven, I was asked to recite a poem at the Christmas celebration in the small town where we lived. I was terrified, but my mother had great confidence in me. However, when I tried to recite the poem before going to the auditorium, I failed miserably.

We rode to the event in silence. All this time, my father had watched and listened, saying nothing. When we got to the auditorium, I was escorted to the steps leading to the stage. Then my father leaned down to me and said, "When you stand up on that stage, don't look at the people. Look at me. I will be in the hallway in the back of the auditorium, behind all the people. You'll be able to see me. The light will be on. You'll see me. Just look at me and tell me the poem."

When the time came, I stood up, and at first I saw only the darkened auditorium of about five hundred people. But then I remembered and looked to the back of the hall. There stood my dad under the only light. I looked at him the whole time and didn't miss a word of the poem. Though there was loud applause, I didn't hear it much at all. I just looked at my dad waving his arms and blowing me a kiss.

Almost sixty-seven years later, that moment still stands out to me. And I learned a powerful lesson about God. My own father, precisely because he loved me, did not remove me from a difficult situation, but he was right there with me. I was not alone! At that point, only God knew how he intended to use me in life and how confidence in speaking would play such a large part in my adult life. *So did I learn, over the years, that God might not take me out of much more difficult situations but that he would be with me with wisdom and encouragement and love.* That is true for all of us, whether we have had good earthly fathers or not. We are *not* fatherless, none of us. We have a Father in heaven. Put your trust in him; you will not be disappointed. Ask your Father in heaven to help you trust him. He wants to give even more than you want to receive.

When I pray the Lord's Prayer, I pray *"Our Father," "my Father," "my Papa."*

"May your name be honored"—not mine.

"May your kingdom come"—not mine. May your kingdom be advanced today in what I think and say and do.

"May your will be done"—not mine.

That's a hard one, but if you ask for God's help, he will eventually show you that his will is better than yours, that doing things his way and according to his will brings a peace, contentment, and joy that will not be taken from you. Start practicing. "Give me today, Papa, my daily bread—not for tomorrow or next week or next year, but for *today*, give me what I need to nourish and sustain myself as I seek to do your will."

This is very important. We are always looking down the road, often in anxiety, for what is coming or for what even *might* be coming. We spend a great deal of energy worrying. Jesus taught each of us, through this prayer, to ask the Father for the bread we need *for today*. He gives us what we need in the moment that we need it. He wants us to put all our trust in him, and that is very hard for us to do. Ask the Holy Spirit for the grace to trust, to rely on the love of God, moment by moment.

"And lead us, lead me, not into temptation." Give me the grace to turn away from things that are opposed to your will.

If we ask God to protect us from serious temptation, then we need to do our part as well. We need to determine which things, people, and activities can or do cause us to sin, and then decide to stay away from them, all the while asking God for the grace to do so. Remember, the Holy Spirit dwells within you; he is present to your every prayer. My earthly father used to say to me, "Put your money where your mouth is." In other words, in a situation that involves temptation, back up your request for God's protection by doing all that *you* can do to avoid those things that regularly lead you into sin.

Sin can be very enticing. That's why we have so much trouble with it. If sin looked ugly, we would naturally avoid it. But sin always looks good. However, it's counterfeit; it won't "pay back" what it promises. Ask God for the grace to see clearly, to see as he does, when you are tempted. Take a deep breath, stand back from the temptation, and ask God to show you the truth. "Give me grace today, my heavenly Father, not to read or to watch or go to Internet sites (insert your own personal areas of temptation) that will lead me into evil. Help me to have the strength to choose the good, to truly be your son or daughter today."

"Deliver me from evil."

Earthly life, in some respects, is an ongoing battle. But don't give in to the tactics of the devil, who lies to you, *especially when you are vulnerable*—that is, in the midst of temptation! Jesus Christ conquered the eternal effects of sin and death for you by dying on the cross. He *will* deliver you from the power of the enemy, but first you must want to be delivered! Some sins we like so much that we call them something else. We rationalize; we try to minimize their effects so that we can continue to enjoy our "sinful pleasures" in secret. The enemy loves to help us keep our sins locked inside. That's when they can do the most damage. If you live a humble, honest life, God will draw very near. He is close to the humble—very close. He will help you and deliver you from evil and give you peace in his kingdom, even here on earth. The battle is lifelong, but those who trust in the Lord will not be disappointed.

> For a day in your courts is better
> than a thousand elsewhere.
> I would rather be a doorkeeper in the house of my God
> than dwell in the tents of wickedness.
> For the LORD God is a sun and shield;
> he bestows favor and honor.
> No good thing does the LORD withhold
> from those who walk uprightly.

O LORD of hosts,
blessed is the man who trusts in you! (Psalm 84:10-12)

"*Amen.*" So be it, by your grace today.

A Father at Work in Your Life

You will notice that I personalized this prayer so that you could more clearly see its application. But Jesus gave us this prayer that we might pray it, not just for ourselves, but for every member of our family, for our friends, and for those with whom we worship, work, and recreate. Jesus taught us how to pray at the apostles' request, but he made clear that even our personal prayer needs to include our brothers and sisters. We are one family in Christ.

If you start praying this way, you open yourself to God's grace. You will see a Father at work in your life as you may not have seen before. Pray this way, in particular, for your spouse. Pray it for your children and grandchildren—each one by name—and watch your Father work on your behalf. Pray this way for close friends. Remember, we do not receive because we do not ask (James 4:2; cf. 1 John 3:22; 5:14).

You have a Father, a real Father, the perfect Father, in heaven. He loves you infinitely more than even the best earthly father could ever love you.

This is an example of how we put ourselves in a place where God can father us. He gave us free will, so we have the power to accept or reject his fatherly care. This prayer is an example of allowing the Holy Spirit, *who is the love between the Father and the Son,* to have full reign in our hearts, our relationships, our crosses, and even our hopes and fears. We have a Father who, by the grace of the Holy Spirit, will draw us into a rich relationship that we did not know was possible. It is the fruit of Baptism!

A good priest in my life said one day, "We go around like orphans. We have a closetful of gifts from our heavenly Father that we have never even opened. In some cases, we haven't even opened the closet door where they sit, sometimes for years." Part of that problem is due to poor catechesis in the Catholic Church in America over the last forty to fifty years. But often another part of that problem is our own lack of faith, as well as our indifference and complacency. Let's make sure the problem doesn't continue in our hearts.

God provides an answer to our cries and needs: his own Spirit. We experienced evidence of that when Blessed John XXIII prayed for a visitation of the Holy Spirit upon the whole Church. Sometimes God's answers don't seem to fit our ideas or plans as to how God should answer us. But look at it this way: God gave us himself, his Spirit, to be our answer. Are we too proud to accept his answer? Are we seeking to control how God chooses to save us, love us, and hear our prayers? If that has been our problem, let us repent! We have a Father in heaven, a Father who created each one of us, who knows what each of us needs more than we ourselves do. Can we humbly accept his gift in the way he chooses to give it?

Do you believe that you have a Father who loves you and that the greatest gift of his love was to give us his Son—his only Son? Many of you reading this book have known the loss of children and grandchildren; there is no pain like it. God your Father gave *his* only Son so that you would not die eternally. His Son suffered for you, to make a way for you, to expiate your sins, if you put your faith in him. That's how much God the Father loves you! Even if you were the only person living, God would have sent his Son to die for you; that's how great your dignity is! You are not just one among billions of people to God; you are unique to God, and he would have sent his Son to die just for you!

As I write this, I can almost hear the doubts. "How could God know each and every one of us?" This is how we often think, because for us it would be impossible; therefore, we tend to think it would be impossible for God as well. But God is infinite; he has no limits. The French philosopher Blaise Pascal once wrote, "God made man in his own image and man returned the compliment." In other words, we fashion God according to a human blueprint and place our human limitations on him. But God has no limits. He can do exactly as he says. He can and does love each one of us uniquely, and he sent his Son to die for *you* and for me! Ask for the faith to believe this; it will change your life. Give the Holy Spirit room to breathe, so to speak, in your life. "You are God's temple and . . . God's Spirit dwells in you" (1 Corinthians 3:16). Start living according to this truth.

Many years ago, my religious community, the Servants of God's Love, discerned that we were being called to bring the love of the Father to those children who were often relegated to the margins of society by poverty and disease. Over the years, we have cared for twenty-six children, two or three at a time, bringing them to live with us. The very first child we received through the state agency was a preemie—a little girl who weighed very little at birth. When we received her into our home, she was just three pounds. On one of the first nights, I was holding her, giving her milk from a tiny, doll-like bottle. We were seated in a rocking chair, and the room was dark. I heard someone call my name from an adjoining room, and I turned my body to respond. When I turned back, I could not find my little girl! She was so small that when I had turned, her little body, enfolded in a blanket, had slipped down between the arm of the chair and my body. Frantically but gently, I pulled up the covers, and there she was, intact! In that moment I actually heard (not audibly), over the pounding of my own heart, the Lord speak: "If she were the only person living on the face of this earth, I would have sent my Son to die—just for her!"

Pope Benedict tells us in his writings that we are, each of us, known individually to God. Each of us is infinitely understood and loved. Each of us is so precious to him that he would spare nothing to save us. But he will never violate our free will. We can choose to reject his love. What a horrible tragedy! Don't let pride keep you from coming to him humbly with your sins and your needs. He will never turn a deaf ear to you. Please take time to read Benedict's first encyclical, *Deus Caritas Est*. What I am saying here is all contained in that encyclical. Take it a section at a time. You can understand it, and it will nourish your soul. You can download it at the Vatican website, www.vatican.va, and read it at your leisure.

We Need a Savior

This Father who loves you gave his only Son to save you from eternal life without God. Do you understand that you *need* to be saved? Many of us faithful Catholics in the pew every Sunday, without realizing it, act more like the Pharisees than disciples.

That's because we tend to think that if we go to Church, try to live by the Ten Commandments, serve at parish events, and contribute to the support of the Church, then we deserve to receive our reward at the end of our earthly lives. But it doesn't work that way. God doesn't keep a kind of report card or auditor's sheet on which are listed our credits and our debits. We think that if our credits outweigh our debits, we go to heaven. We imagine a report card where there are few Fs and a lot of As and Bs and think, "That should get me there." But again, we have tried to put a human construct on an infinite reality.

God wants a relationship with us. That's why he created us. That's why he gave *his only Son* to suffer torment—to expiate the sins of our first parents and open for us the gates of heaven. Do you believe this?

Ask yourself these questions: How deep is my faith, really? How much does God's word form my daily thoughts, words, and actions? Do I see myself as a son or daughter of the Father? Do I daily ask God for the grace of his Spirit to guide me to overcome my faults and failings and to forgive me when I fail? Do I make frequent use of the Sacrament of Reconciliation in order to face my sins and failings and to receive life-giving grace to *change*?

There's the key. When I am living my life in such a way that I am growing closer to God, conforming my life to his grace, those who see me, a son or daughter of God, will see more and more of Jesus in me and through me. That's what the Father wants. That's why Jesus died for us—so that the Spirit could come and lead us into all truth. God your Father wants to see the family resemblance in you. It's not a matter of debits and credits; this is not some kind of business transaction. This is the Father, with infinite love for you and me, giving us superabundant grace to die to ourselves by giving up our sin so that we can become more and more like him! We cannot accomplish that, no matter how many good deeds we perform. We can't earn it. In this way, we receive our eternal inheritance, our baptismal identity, and live as his sons and daughters in this world so that many will be attracted to him—not to us, but to him! When we yield our lives to the Holy Spirit who dwells within us, God will respond to our generosity by making us more and more like his Son.

It is not easy to let go of our own will, to do things God's way, but the result is hope and confidence in this life and everlasting happiness in the next. This is not a pipe dream; this is reality. Don't live your life like an accountant. Enter into the life of love God has for you—the life Jesus Christ made possible for you by his death on the cross.

And the price we pay for such a life? That I freely admit that I cannot save myself, that I need a savior. That I freely confess my sins that dim or obliterate God's presence in my life. That I stop keeping a debit/credit ledger and surrender to the love of God present within me by the Holy Spirit. This is the same Holy Spirit who is always seeking to return to the Father in me, with me, day by day leading me into the presence of the Father, to be taught and strengthened, to be challenged and nourished, and to more and more reflect the image of Jesus. Again, this is not pious imagery. This is the reality of our lives. By the grace of Baptism, the Holy Spirit dwells within us to empower us to be all that God created us to be: his true sons and daughters!

Many years ago, when Confession face-to-face was first introduced, I went to a priest who knew me well. It was the first time I had gone to Confession face-to-face. I had mentally prepared a list of my sins, and when I finished my list of sins, the priest put his head in his hands. I could see his lips moving, so I knew that he was praying. In my complacency and stupidity, I wondered why. All he had to do was give me absolution; I had fulfilled my part, hadn't I? After a few minutes—a very long few minutes, it seemed—he lifted his head and asked, "Sister, are you sorry for *anything* you have just confessed?" Stunned by the question, I was ready to answer in righteous indignation, "Well, of course I am! I wouldn't be here if I wasn't."

But something stopped me, and in a moment of unusual clarity, I realized I wasn't truly repentant. If I had been truly sorry when I went to Confession, I would have been working to overcome, by grace, the root causes of my sin. Instead, I just kept confessing the same sins over and over. Yes, God would forgive me, but if I were truly sorry, wouldn't there be some change? If I were really sorry, wouldn't I do my best to alter my behavior? If I really loved God, wouldn't I try to speak and act in a way that manifested that love? I wasn't trying. In a way, I was presuming on God's mercy and not taking responsibility for my need to change. That confession changed my life, and for the first time I began to understand that God my Father had given me his Son to lead me safely home—a Son who would make a way for me, who would be my Shepherd and my Savior.

I spent four months going before the tabernacle daily, asking God to show me how much I stood in need of his mercy. Some days I went hourly. I realized that, in spite of all my good deeds,

I still couldn't save myself! It was a huge blow to my pride, but the result was that my Savior became my personal Savior. By the power of the Holy Spirit, I learned that my willingness to admit my absolute inability to save myself brought me almost literally into the arms of Jesus. For the first time, I truly realized that I was created for union with God, the Source of all beauty, all truth, and all love. My hunger, my thirst for God increased; these first fruits were all the work of the Holy Spirit. Jesus was there, present to me, by the love of the Father, shepherding me, saving me, and leading me home. The Holy Spirit desires to do that for each of us. His action in each of our lives is unique, but the goal is the same: to bring us safely home to God forever!

Another great truth that became evident for me after I was prayed with to open myself to the gifts of the Holy Spirit was this: the Holy Spirit *is* the love between the Father and the Son. That love is so infinite that it "generates" the third Person of the Blessed Trinity. I may be a bit clumsy in the use of certain words, but the reality is that eternal Love, dwelling in us through Baptism, seeks to lead us to union with the Father and the Son by the power of that Love, the Holy Spirit! I know it's mind-boggling: you and I are called to union with God! It is for this purpose that we were created. It is the answer to all the longings and desires inside of us. We were created to live eternally in union with God!

God the Father, God the Son, God the Holy Spirit: we need a relationship with all three Persons of the Blessed Trinity, one God, if we are going to be true disciples.

Chapter Six

Activating the Gifts of Baptism and Confirmation

In the midst of writing this book, I was invited to the baptism of four children. The deacon presiding over the baptisms is a marvelous teacher, and he explained every part of the ceremony. Speaking of the beauty of the day, he talked about how good it was to see parents of real faith gathered for the celebration of the sacrament. But, he said, no matter how beautiful were the things that we could see, there was a far greater reality, a far greater beauty being presented. These children, he said, are receiving the fruits of Jesus' death on the cross. They are receiving the very presence of God in their souls through the Holy Spirit. They are being radically changed into sons and daughters of the eternal Father. The enemy is being cast out from their midst. Gifts of priceless, eternal value are being bestowed.

The mothers and the fathers of the children, in the blessing of the parents, were exhorted and counseled to lead their children to an understanding of what was being given to them in this moment: the hope and the promise of eternal life to those who would follow God. The godparents and the grandparents also received a strong exhortation to lead these little ones to Christ.

In the baptismal ceremony, we can become so focused on the child, the candle, the dress, the pictures, the gifts, or the friends that we give no thought to what is actually happening. But the

Catechism of the Catholic Church tells us, "The fruit of the sacramental life is that the Spirit of adoption makes the faithful *partakers in the divine nature by uniting them in a living union with the only Son, the Savior*" (1129, emphasis mine). In Confirmation we are confirmed as disciples of Christ, followers of Jesus who seek the gifts that will enable us both to identify with Christ more deeply and to serve the people of God with the gifts we receive from him.

A deeper understanding of these sacraments is absolutely necessary. The gifts given to us in Baptism and Confirmation are more fully activated by God's generous sharing of his life and by our assent to the action of the living God in our souls—our definite and personal yes to Christian discipleship. This is essentially what is meant by the "baptism in the Holy Spirit." We are not being rebaptized; that is not possible. It is simply that we now understand more thoroughly the gifts we have received, and we seek to activate them in our lives through our personal understanding and assent to the grace God is offering us.

The Gifts Bestowed at Baptism

When the cleansing waters of Baptism washed over you, *something very real happened.* The sin inherited from Adam and Eve was removed from you. The blood of Christ on the cross was the payment for your redemption. You were washed clean *and* you were given the first pledge of your eternal inheritance, the Holy Spirit: "He has put his seal upon us and given us his Spirit in our hearts as a guarantee" (2 Corinthians 1:22). You became a temple of the Holy Spirit! "Do you not know that you are God's temple and that God's Spirit dwells in you?" (1 Corinthians 3:16). This really happened; it is not just pious imagery.

The *Catechism* tells us the following:

> Baptism not only purifies from all sins, but also makes the neophyte "a new creature," an adopted son of God, who has become a "partaker of the divine nature," member of Christ and co-heir with him, and a temple of the Holy Spirit. (1265)

> The Most Holy Trinity gives the baptized sanctifying grace, the grace of *justification:* enabling them to believe in God, to hope in him, and to love him through the theological virtues; giving them the power to live and act under the prompting of the Holy Spirit through the gifts of the Holy Spirit; allowing them to grow in goodness through the moral virtues. Thus the whole organism of the Christian's supernatural life has its roots in Baptism. (1266)

> Baptism makes us members of the Body of Christ. (1267)

> The baptized have become "living stones." (1268)

> The person baptized belongs no longer to himself, but to him who died and rose for us. (1269)

By the power of the Holy Spirit, Baptism lays the solid foundation for a personal relationship with God as we mature, but it requires good instruction and personal example by those in the child's life. The *Catechism* states this very strongly:

> For the grace of Baptism to unfold, the parents' help is important. So too is the role of the *godfather* and *godmother*, who must be firm believers, able and ready to help the newly baptized—child or adult—on the road of Christian life. . . . The whole ecclesial community bears some responsibility for the development and safeguarding of the grace given at Baptism. (1255)

Parents and godparents, take your role seriously—above all, through prayer and example, using words only when necessary! Children need counsel, wisdom, and fortitude to live a full life as God intended. How sad it is that we provide them with all the material blessings we can afford, such as unprecedented educational opportunities beyond high school and all the medical care available to secure their health, but we give little or no concern to what will last forever: their immortal souls! The enemy has done a great job on us: we who for several generations have had the best academic education in the world do not know or understand the most important realities of life.

Frankly, I don't see this understanding of Baptism at work in most families and parishes. With the diminution of active faith all across parishes in the U.S., many Catholics treat the sacrament as a nice ceremony at best and, with greater frequency today, simply ignore its place in the lives of their children. If we don't understand who we are and the grace imparted to us in

Baptism, how can we help that grace to develop and safeguard it in those for whom we are responsible?

Notice above what the *Catechism* says: that the baptized person *"belongs no longer to himself, but to him who died and rose for us"* (1269, emphasis mine). Look at your life now. Do you know who you are? Do you know why you were created? Are you cooperating with the grace given you by the Holy Spirit? Can you proclaim with St. Paul: "It is no longer I who live, but Christ who lives in me; and the life I now live in the flesh I live by faith in the Son of God, who loved me and gave himself for me" (Galatians 2:20)?

Many years ago, I was asked to be godmother for a baby yet to be born. For many weeks I prayed for that child. When the mother came home from the hospital, I eagerly went to the house to meet this child for whom I had prayed. From the moment I stepped on the porch, I could hear the baby screaming. I entered to find a mother exhausted from trying to care for a child that seemed inconsolable. As I held this child and looked at her, I detected all the signs of great anger. "How is this possible," I thought, "that a baby five days old could be angry?" But, fairly strongly convinced of it, I approached the mother, who had already exhausted all the possible physical causes with their doctor. I prayed for sensitivity and then asked, "Would there be any reason why your baby could be angry?" This dear, dear mother looked up at me and whispered, "Sister, we didn't want this baby; we can't afford her." I was so grateful that she could be honest. I asked her if she and her husband would go to Confession to get the burden of fear and helplessness off their backs and their souls. They did. The following Sunday, during Mass, this child was baptized. As I held her, she continued to scream, but when the priest prayed the prayers of exorcism over that child during the baptismal rite, he prayed specifically that any spirit of rejection would be gone. When the waters of Baptism covered her little body, she stopped crying immediately!

There is power, real power, in this sacrament to set us free from the effects of sin inherited from our first parents, Adam and Eve, and from anything a child may have inherited from his mother and father.

Baptism is no symbolic rite. It is a gift from God to set us free and to make us his sons and daughters, able to inherit the gift of eternal life. The Holy Spirit is given to each of us in Baptism as the first pledge of our inheritance.

This is a gift given by God in which he seeks to draw us personally—yes, each one of us, yes, *you*—into union with him. As we mature through the work of the Holy Spirit, we begin, if we are well instructed, to place God's priorities above our own. God gives us the grace and strength to let go of certain sins, and in place of those sins, he fills us with his desires and hopes. He conforms us to himself and, in doing so, draws us into union with the Source of all love! The gifts outlined above are God's sharing his very self with us—not just good things that God likes to share, but God giving us *himself!* He comes that near. But we have free will; we can say no.

God desires an intimate personal relationship with each of us. These gifts that make us like him, that identify us with him, have a price. The price is giving up our will to do things our way for our own satisfaction; it is giving up the right to tell

God what we want and when we want it. It is giving up even the right that comes with free will to tell God how we are going to be his disciple!

The Gifts Bestowed at Confirmation

Now, as a baptized person with the rights and privileges mentioned in the *Catechism*, let us look at what the *Catechism* says in section 1303 about the gifts we receive in Confirmation:

Confirmation brings an increase and deepening of baptismal grace: it roots us more deeply in the divine filiation [sons and daughters] which makes us cry, "Abba! Father!"; it unites us more firmly to Christ; it increases the gifts of the Holy Spirit in us; it renders our bond with the Church more perfect; it gives us a special strength of the Holy Spirit to spread and defend the faith by word and action as true witnesses of Christ, to confess the name of Christ boldly, and never to be ashamed of the Cross:

"Recall then that you have received the spiritual seal, the spirit of wisdom and understanding, the spirit of right judgment and courage, the spirit of knowledge and reverence, the spirit of holy fear in God's presence. Guard what you have received. God the Father has marked you with his sign; Christ the Lord has confirmed you and has placed his pledge, the Spirit, in your hearts" (St. Ambrose, *De myst.* 7, 42: PL 16, 402–403).

Read that description carefully again. Are you experiencing an increase of gifts in your life as you follow the Lord? You should be, but don't be discouraged if you aren't. Just keep reading.

Let's take an even closer look at the gifts God gave us as baptized and confirmed Catholics.

First, look at the gifts enumerated in Isaiah 11:2-3. Were they taught to you, through instruction in CCD programs or in Catholic schools, in a way that made you seek them? I would say that we made a mistake in the Charismatic Renewal by focusing first on the gifts for service found in 1 Corinthians 12–14, which are essential gifts in building up the body of Christ and equipping disciples. However, I think there are other gifts that should have taken priority that we did not sufficiently take into account to equip us for lifelong discipleship and ministry.

In April through June of 1989, Pope John Paul II devoted his Sunday Regina Caeli and Angelus messages to speaking about the gifts of wisdom, understanding, counsel, fortitude, knowledge, piety, and fear of the Lord that Isaiah described. These are gifts beyond price because they conform us to God in Christ; they make us like him, draw us into union with him, and empower us to reflect his will. Growing in Christ is a lifelong endeavor; nevertheless, the power of God's Spirit enables us to identify with God, to become one with God as God himself desires. Every good human father rejoices to see his children reflecting his good qualities and characteristics. Our heavenly Father wants to powerfully pour out on us those gifts that most make us like him! In turn, we can use these gifts to grow deeper in our union with God so that we will reflect his will and purpose in the world around us.

For the purpose of this book, let me summarize these gifts of the Holy Spirit using John Paul's own words. But I urge you to go online and read the complete texts.

> On this Second Sunday of Easter [April 2, 1989] throughout the entire Church the words which the Risen Christ addressed to the apostles on the night of his resurrection resound, words which are both a gift and a promise: "Receive the Holy Spirit" (John 20:23). . . . The Resurrection completely fulfilled the Redeemer's saving plan, the limitless outpouring of divine love upon humanity. It is now up to the Spirit to involve individuals in that plan of love. . . . "The spirit of him who raised Jesus from the dead" (Romans 8:11) must dwell in us and lead us to a life which is more and more conformed to that of the risen Christ.[1]

> **Wisdom** . . . is a light which we receive from on high; it is a special sharing in that mysterious and highest knowledge which is that of God himself. . . . This higher wisdom is the root of a new awareness, a knowledge permeated by charity, by means of which the soul becomes familiar, so to say, with divine things, and tastes them. St. Thomas speaks precisely of "a certain taste of God," through which the truly wise person is not simply one who knows the things of God but rather the one who experiences and lives them. . . . [It] further gives us a special ability to judge human things according to God's standard, in God's light.[2]

Understanding. Through this gift the Holy Spirit who "sees into the depths of God" (1 Corinthians 2:10), communicates to the believer a glint of such a penetrating capacity, opening the heart to the joyous understanding of God's loving plan. . . . This supernatural intelligence is given not only to individuals, but also to the community: to pastors who, as successors of the Apostles, are heirs to the specific promise made to them by Christ (cf. John 14:26; 16:13), and to the faithful who, thanks to the "anointing" of the Spirit (cf. 1 John 2:20 and 27), possess a special "sense of the faith" (*sensus fidei*) which guides them in their concrete choices. The light of the Spirit, in fact, while it sharpens the understanding of divine things, renders ever more clear and penetrating the understanding of human things.[3]

Counsel. It is given to the Christian to enlighten the conscience in moral choices which daily life presents. . . . The gift of Counsel acts like a new breath in the conscience, suggesting to it what is licit, what is becoming, what is more fitting for the soul. . . . Thus the conscience becomes like the "healthy eye," . . . an eye which acquires, as it were, a new pupil, by means of which it is able to see better what to do in a given situation, no matter how intricate and difficult.[4]

Fortitude. In our time many extol physical force, to the extent of also approving the extreme forms of violence. In fact, man has daily experience of his own weakness, especially in the spiritual and moral sphere, yielding to the impulses of internal passions and external pressures. Precisely to resist these multiple stimuli, it is necessary to have the virtue of fortitude. . . . It is the virtue by which one does not compromise in fulfilling one's duty. . . . The gift of Fortitude is a supernatural impulse which gives strength to the soul, not only on exceptional occasions such as that of martyrdom, but also in normal difficulties: in the struggle to remain consistent with one's principles; in putting up with insults and unjust attacks; in courageous perseverance on the path of truth and uprightness, in spite of lack of understanding and hostility.[5]

Knowledge. Before the manifold magnificence of things, their complexity, variety, and beauty, [man] runs the risk of absolutizing and almost divinizing them to the extent of making them the supreme purpose of his very life. This happens especially when it is a matter of riches, pleasure, and power, which indeed can be drawn from material things. . . . In order to resist such subtle temptations and to remedy the pernicious consequences to which they can lead, the Holy Spirit aids people with the gift of Knowledge. It is this gift which helps them to value things correctly in their essential dependence on the Creator.[6]

Piety. With [this gift], the Spirit heals our hearts of every form of hardness, and opens them to tenderness towards

God and our brothers and sisters. . . . The experience of one's own existential poverty, of the void which earthly things leave in the soul, gives rise to the need to have recourse to God in order to obtain grace, help, and pardon. The gift of piety directs and nourishes such need, enriching it with sentiments of profound confidence in God; trusted as a good and generous Father. . . . Tenderness, an authentically fraternal openness towards one's neighbor, is manifested in meekness. With the gift of piety the Spirit infuses into the believer a new capacity for love of the brethren. . . . [It] further extinguishes in the heart those fires of tension and division which are bitterness, anger and impatience, and nourishes feelings of understanding, tolerance, and pardon.[7]

Fear of the Lord. [This gift] certainly is not that "fear of God" which causes people to flee from every thought and memory of him, as something or someone who disturbs and upsets. . . . It is a sincere and reverential feeling that a person experiences before the tremendous majesty of God. . . . The believer goes and places himself before God with a "contrite spirit" and a "humbled heart" (cf. Psalm 50:19). . . . The soul is now concerned not to displease God, whom he loves as a Father, not to offend him in anything, to "abide in him" and grow in charity (cf. John 15:4-7).[8]

One comment I would like to make about the gift of knowledge: we often determine the truth of what someone says by what *we* see and hear, that is, by the information that our senses give us. We hear how other people speak of a person or a situation, we consider their opinions and viewpoints, and then we tend to make a judgment. We may read a book or an article or consult scientific experts, should the decision warrant it; or we may consult the Internet for information and then make a decision. We tend to think our decision is a good one, a mature one. After all, we didn't just react to something; we're not making a decision based simply on anger or fear. So all in all, we feel justified and can even call our decision "mature" and "reasoned."

But as a follower of Christ, we are forgetting one major area—the most important one. Have we consulted God? Have we placed our thoughts, our reasoning, before him? God wants to show us how he sees things. When we are dealing with a difficult situation, it is fine to consult experts in the field, but it is first necessary to consult God! If we do, God will show us how important this issue is in light of eternity. How does the decision I make now affect my eternal destiny, the destiny of those around me? What eternal values are at stake here?

We want God to have first place in our thoughts, words, and deeds. That means we need to call on the gift of knowledge when we are confused about priorities, relations with others, and the importance of those relationships in light of God's plan for us on this earth. In our world, two criteria often hold highest priority: our emotions and the scientific findings of other "experts" in the field we are discussing. Those two we put on a pedestal. This is a mistake. Put first the knowledge of who you are, to whom you belong, and what the purpose of your life is. Then ask yourself, "In light of those answers, how do I deal with the

circumstances and decisions before me on a day-to-day basis?"
I guarantee this gift will bring you clarity and peace of mind and
heart as you seek for answers in your area of concern.

The Life of a Disciple

God did not give us these gifts for ourselves; he did not give
his Spirit so that we could consider ourselves privileged and special. God gave the gift of his Spirit in our Baptism so that we
might belong to the family of God as sons and daughters. He
gave his Spirit so that we might be his disciples in a world that
is searching for purpose and meaning. He gave his Spirit so that
we might be the light of truth and love in the darkness of profound confusion. He gave his Spirit so that as we walk through
this valley of darkness, we might fear no evil but be empowered to be the light of Christ: the light of faith, hope, and love.

I have known people who have carried these gifts with reverence and gratitude even to the end of their lives, as disciples are
called to do. Let me tell you a few remarkable stories.

The first one is about a married woman who, with her husband, had been faithful to God's call by raising their children
well, even though this woman was ill for many years. They were
involved in the Catholic Charismatic Renewal for many years and
were good stewards of the gifts that God had given them. Nothing
stopped them from praising God and seeking to follow him more
closely every day. The conversations I had with the wife, often
on the phone, attested to her strong Christian character and her
great virtue and were confirmed by her husband. When she was
suffering a great deal and knew that God was calling her home

to himself, after talking to her children, she asked to meet with *each* of her twenty-four grandchildren individually. She spoke to each grandchild, reminding them of who they are—sons and daughters of God—and of the gifts they had received from God, and advising them how to use those gifts. She encouraged each one to foster the life of the Holy Spirit in their hearts and minds and to grow in their Catholic faith. One by one, said other family members, each grandchild came out of the hospital room with tears and a smile, simultaneously. One college-aged grandchild said to me some weeks after the grandmother's death, "I walked out of that hospital room feeling like I had been given a legacy." That, brothers and sisters, is living out your baptismal promises in the power of the Holy Spirit. That's the fruit of God's gift being nurtured by a woman of solid Catholic faith with others in her family, parish, and prayer group through the years.

Several years ago, someone called my office, asking if she could have some copies of my booklet *Hope in the Midst of Suffering.*[9] This woman was in a nursing home; she had read my booklet and had been encouraged. She told me so many of the residents were hopeless, and she wanted to encourage them. I quickly sent her a number of the booklets, and she distributed them and encouraged those who accepted the booklet. This is the fruit of the baptism in the Holy Spirit: in spite of her own need and loneliness, this woman was enabled to comfort others with the same consolation she had received from the Spirit.

A social worker called my office one day and said that she worked in a hospice facility in Louisiana. A patient there was dying of cancer and had asked this social worker to call me and see if she could get copies of one of my booklets for every person in that hospice facility. The social worker said she would pay for them if I would send them quickly. I did. Here again was a woman who could have been understandably focused on herself but was evangelizing even to the end, which in turn had a real impact on the social worker. That is the power of the Holy Spirit working in us, who can do far more than we could ask or imagine.

An elderly African-American man contacted me from a major city on the East Coast. "Sister, I am almost blind now. I can't go out anymore, but I can invite people into my home to watch a good DVD. Could you tell me what you have that would be good? I want to give them the truth; I want to give them hope. They need Jesus!"

All of these people, some even in the last days of their lives, were burning with the fire of the Holy Spirit, thinking of others rather than of themselves, seeking to give rather than to receive. Where does that power come from? From the Holy Spirit who dwells within us.

Through Renewal Ministries I have seen countless people who have sacrificed time, money, comfort, and convenience to bring the gospel to brothers and sisters in many poverty-stricken countries in the world.

I have seen young people from our local Catholic high school give up vacation time at Christmas and Easter to travel with adults to poverty-stricken areas—young people who returned with literally nothing but the clothes on their backs. They gave away everything they had brought with them—without even a suggestion from the adults. Those young people are catching fire from adults who have known the power of the Holy Spirit and have willingly shared their living faith in Jesus Christ. I spoke to one young man who had just returned. "How was it?" I asked. "I've been branded for life," he replied.

All of these stories are true, and they are possible because each person was led to or is drinking from the fount of living water. They are true disciples, some still novices, but they all know that the Holy Spirit is real; they know that he is the source of wisdom, strength, and love. They have been branded by his fire.

About six years ago, a young man in our parish asked me if I would be his Confirmation sponsor. Such a commitment requires the sponsor to accompany that person on his journey by meeting frequently, giving witness to God's gifts at work in his life, and encouraging his full entrance into the Church through prayer and example. In our first meeting, I asked this young man, "Why do you want to be confirmed?" Immediately came a quiet but confident answer: "Because I want to be a fully equipped disciple of Jesus Christ." And best of all, in the six years since his Confirmation, he is living out that desire in daily life. That is the power of the Holy Spirit.

Too often, I think, in today's world, especially in North America and Western Europe, we have too many options, too many possibilities in a wide variety of areas. Our young people actually are stymied by all these options and can't make decisions—because they might miss out on something—and sometimes they even become paralyzed and just drift. Young people today need models: adults who have the right priorities, who have placed Jesus Christ first in their lives, no matter their vocation, and have sold all, so to speak, to be his disciples. Such adults can become light in the darkness for all these young people today.

If you were, or are, part of the Charismatic Renewal, does the presence of the Holy Spirit lead your daily life, your decisions, your relationships, and your goals in life? If you had asked the Holy Spirit to be activated in your life and had placed your life at his disposal, and he then gifted you, you now have a responsibility to use those gifts. At the end of your life, you will be called to render an account. Are you ready to do so? So many young people today declare that they have no religion to which they belong, no belief in God. *They need you.*

A Marvelous Opportunity

According to a recent survey by the Pew Research Center's Forum on Religion and Public Life,

> The growth in the number of religiously unaffiliated Americans—sometimes called the rise of the "nones"—is largely driven by generational replacement, the gradual supplanting of older generations by newer ones. A third of adults under thirty have no religious affiliation, compared with just one in ten who are sixty-five and older. And young adults today are much more likely to be unaffiliated than previous generations were at a similar stage in their lives.[10]

In addition,

> The number of Americans who do not identify with any religion continues to grow at a rapid pace. . . . In the

last five years alone, the unaffiliated have increased from just over 15 percent to just under 20 percent of all U.S. adults. Their ranks now include more than 13 million self-described atheists and agnostics (nearly 6 percent of the U.S. public), as well as nearly 33 million people who say they have no particular religious affiliation.[11]

As "one nation under God," we are in trouble. We need not point the finger in blame, but we do need to ask ourselves what we can do to turn this around. I think we have a marvelous opportunity to open ourselves to God's grace so that he, by the work of his Holy Spirit, can form us more deeply into real disciples and make us truly useful for his purposes.

Again, I would say that we made a mistake in the Charismatic Renewal in focusing first on the gifts for service found in 1 Corinthians 12–14. They are essential gifts for building up the body of Christ and equipping disciples; nevertheless, each Catholic man or woman needs to know who they *are* before they can use the gifts given to them to serve others. I think that in some ways we put the cart before the horse, assuming that most of us had been well catechized and knew what it meant to be a baptized and confirmed Catholic. Sadly, we did not. There are inestimable gifts from Baptism and Confirmation.

We always taught in the Catholic Charismatic Renewal that baptism in the Holy Spirit was a prayer, first, to activate the gifts we had already received in Baptism and Confirmation and, then, to equip us for service in the body of Christ. But unfortunately, most of us had separated the knowledge gained in Catholic schools and CCD programs from daily life, with its challenges and trials. As a result, the gifts given in these sacraments lay dormant for many years because of a lack of understanding of how to apply those gifts to everyday living. God will never force us to enter into a deeper relationship with him. He will never force us to use our gifts to benefit our brothers and sisters. We have been given the "awe-full" gift of free will. God puts treasures in our laps, even lavishly, but we have to decide, to make the choice, to use them for his glory! We have to decide to make a relationship with God, with his Son Jesus, and with the Holy Spirit the first priority of our lives, no matter what our state in life.

A basic discipleship commitment has to take place in being confirmed. We cannot assume it is there just because we have taught it. Have we truly taught it? Have we modeled it? Do young people about to be confirmed in the Church see disciples all around them on whom they can model themselves? Do they understand the priority of Christian discipleship? The answer is clear. The majority of Catholics do not know what it means to be a disciple of Christ, and in many cases those who call themselves Catholics have no evident desire to take up their cross and follow him.

Gifts beyond Price

Are these gifts received through Baptism and Confirmation really operating in our lives? If they are, then our personal relationship with God should be growing. On our own, we cannot fully assess that—only God can—but we can ask if there is fruit being borne in our lives, the fruits of faith, hope, and love for him and for his people. Do I reach out to those in need? Do I seek to spend more time with him when I can? Am I hungry for his word, for the sacraments? Do I prioritize them over my own personal desires? Am I confident in his presence in the midst of life's daily challenges? Do I turn to him often throughout the day? Do I spend time in worship and thanksgiving? Do I take the initiative to mend fences when needed? Do I quickly admit my mistakes?

God wants a people—and each individual—to have a personal relationship with him, not, first of all, in order to safeguard the gifts of service, but in order that each one of us may know in mind and heart to whom we belong. By the light of his face, he wants to burn off the darkness of sin and error in body and mind; by the power of his Spirit dwelling in us, he wants to purify our self-centeredness until we can put him in first place in our thoughts and then in our words and actions. He wants to shift the center of our gravity from self to him. He seeks union with us, but it has to be on his terms. He gives us gifts, but we have to use those gifts in conformity to his will. That's what makes the fruit of those gifts possible; he gives us everything we need to love and serve him. *But* each of us has to give God time to work that transformation in our minds, our bodies, and our spirits.

Let me repeat the verses from Mark's Gospel that I cited in chapter 3:

And he went up on the mountain, and called to him those whom he desired; and they came to him. And he appointed twelve, to be with him, and to be sent out to preach and have authority to cast out demons. (Mark 3:13-15)

As I stressed earlier, the personal relationship of Jesus with his Father is of first importance, even in the midst of many needs. In communication with his Father, Jesus retreats to a nearby mountain to pray. This time he calls "those whom he desired" to come with him. Those closest to him, those whom the Father had told him to gather, *he called them to be with him! Not first to do*—anything!—but to *be* with him! That is an extremely significant verse for present-day disciples. Only when we spend time with Jesus—waste time, it may seem to the world, to walk with Jesus and to be with him—do we receive his wisdom, courage, and trust in the Father. Only when we spend time with Jesus do we find a quiet place in his heart to be restored by his grace! Not first and foremost to *do* anything but to be with him, to receive from him the gifts he knows we need. It takes time to see our sin and repent, to give up our own will, to grow in love so that I matter less and less and he matters more and more. Jesus was looking for friends, for close companions to whom he could give his love and share himself. He placed that above the needs of the poor. Only when the first disciples were really converted and walked in intimate fellowship with him could he trust them with his gifts. That would come with the Holy Spirit. Even then the disciples would have much to learn—and one among them would never learn.

Again, I repeat, and hear me, please! It is precisely here that I think we made an understandable mistake, but a mistake nonetheless, in the Charismatic Renewal as a movement. We put doing before being—doing service before being fully committed as an intimate friend and disciple. When the first flush of anointing passed, so to speak, many drifted away for other, more "exciting things."

Erasmo Leiva-Merikakis, a Scripture scholar and now a monk known as Brother Simeon, has a marvelous commentary on Mark's Gospel (especially 3:14-15) wherein he underscores the lesson from this passage for us as disciples: the need for an ever-developing relationship with Christ through daily prayer, because our relationship with him, our intimacy with Jesus, always has to have first place.[12] It is in that ongoing, deepening relationship that the gifts we have been given can be used to reveal Christ to those in need! The poor need a savior. The gifts are intended to lead them closer to Christ. The gifts and their fruit should lead every healed and delivered person to deeper trust in Christ. Only through an ongoing relationship with God can we use the gifts with power and according to his plan!

Again, it is logical to say that in every encounter with God, God is not as concerned with what we do for him and for the building of his kingdom as with who we are and what kind of relationship we have with Jesus, to whom we can introduce those who come to us for prayer and healing.

So how do we become more his disciples so that we can be good stewards of the graces he has given us? *We need more of the Holy Spirit,* and we need to treat the gift of his graces with greater reverence. We are only the stewards, not the owners!

CHAPTER SEVEN

Three More Gifts: Faith, Hope, and Love

It's important to discuss three more gifts that every disciple needs: faith, hope, and love. We have talked about these theological virtues in this book under different headings, but I want us to focus on them now in their own right. That's because, in a very particular way, these three virtues, when they are developed in our lives, lead us to directly reflect Christ—the goal of every true disciple.

The theological virtues relate directly to God. "They are infused by God into the souls of the faithful to make them capable of acting as his children and of meriting eternal life" (*Catechism of the Catholic Church*, 1813). This happens through Baptism and Confirmation. They are the pledge of the presence and action of the Holy Spirit in the faculties of the human being. The definition of "virtue" is "an habitual and firm disposition to do the good" (*Catechism*, 1803). The theological virtues dispose Christians to live in a relationship with the Holy Trinity. So these are not just a list of sterile truths that you memorize and try to live by; these are the gifts that bring you into a living relationship with God himself.

Faith

"Faith is the theological virtue by which we believe in God and believe all that he has said and revealed to us, and that Holy Church proposes for our belief, *because he is truth itself*" (*Catechism*, 1814; emphasis mine).

The seed of faith is planted by Baptism, but it has to be watered and nourished. So many people say to me, "Well, I just don't have faith." Any gardener knows that light, food, and water are essential to the growth of a seed—and so should we! The seed *is* there. Our souls need the light of God's truth and his presence through his word. We need to be nourished, not only by God's word, but most of all by the food of the Eucharist. Many of us, on a spiritual level, operate on a starvation diet. So of course we will be weak! No seed will bear good fruit if its soil is barren. We also need water—the life-giving water of Baptism and Confirmation flowing into our souls daily. We need to consent with our will to allow the inspirations and convictions of the Holy Spirit to penetrate our minds and to guide our decisions.

Daily we are confronted by sin, darkness, anger, bitterness, and even hatred. Daily we are confronted by violence, greed, and jealousy. Their presence and effects can damage the soil of our minds and hearts, making it rocky or sandy, and thus the seed is starved. The overall effect, then, is to weaken a sense of who we are and of where we are going. We need to ask for greater faith! Daily I personally try to do that simply by asking God to increase my faith: "Give me eyes to see and ears to hear what you are about that I might follow you." Or you can us this very simple prayer: "Lord, increase my faith!" You can certainly pray in your own words, but do ask daily.

Hope

"Hope is the theological virtue by which we desire the kingdom of heaven and eternal life as our happiness, placing our trust in Christ's promises and relying not on our own strength, but on the help of the grace of the Holy Spirit. 'Let us hold fast the confession of our hope without wavering, for he who promised is faithful' (Hebrews 10:23)" (*Catechism*, 1817).

The virtue of hope helps us to put our confidence and trust in the right place. How many times have we "hoped" for something, only to be severely disappointed? Much of that comes simply because we live in an imperfect world, and many people and situations can disappoint us—sometimes terribly—especially if someone gave us reason to hope, only to find that they were lying or had no intention of fulfilling what they had promised.

But, brothers and sisters, God is different. When God promises, *he delivers!* That is why we can hope in him for the fulfillment of all that he has promised. God never lies; he will never lead us astray if we follow him, even (and especially) when times are hard and we can't see the fulfillment of our hopes.

Many times we use the word "hope" when we really mean "wishful thinking"; it is usually not based on God's promises. For example, I "hope" it will be a nice day tomorrow for the picnic. I don't have control over the weather, so my hope is actually the expression of a wish—a good wish, but not one of which any of us can promise the result. We might say, "I hope

I get the job" or "I hope I get a good grade on this project." In these cases, there is some personal involvement because we need to do our part to hone our skills and abilities. But still, we cannot control the outcome. We can "hope," but the success lies outside our sphere of control.

Now, when we are talking about the theological virtue of hope, we are talking about something very different. God has made promises to us, and he is true to his word! There is no place here for wishful thinking. God's promises are true. He *is* truth itself. You can absolutely depend on the truth of his word. Again, look at Scripture: "No distrust made [Abraham] waver concerning the promise of God, but he grew strong in his faith as he gave glory to God, fully convinced that God was able to do what he had promised" (Romans 4:20-21).

What are God's promises to us? I cannot list them all here, but here are a few promises that Jesus made to his disciples. Remember that you and I are called to be his disciples, so these promises are for us as well.

"In my Father's house are many rooms; if it were not so, would I have told you that I go to prepare a place for you? And when I go and prepare a place for you, I will come again and will take you to myself, that where I am you may be also. . . . I am the way, and the truth, and the life; no one comes to the Father, but by me." (John 14:2-3, 6)

"Truly, truly, I say to you, he who believes in me will also do the works that I do; and greater works than these will he do, because I go to the Father. Whatever you ask in my name, I will do it, that the Father may be glorified in the Son. If you ask anything in my name, I will do it. "If you love me, you will keep my commandments. And I will ask the Father, and he will give you another Counselor, to be with you for ever, even the Spirit of truth, whom the world cannot receive, because it neither sees him nor knows him; you know him, for he dwells with you, and will be in you." (John 14:12-17)

"These things I have spoken to you, while I am still with you. But the Counselor, the Holy Spirit, whom the Father will send in my name, he will teach you all things, and bring to your remembrance all that I have said to you." (John 14:25-26)

If you have faith, these promises should engender in you real hope. If your faith is weak, read and pray over these promises, letting them take root in your soul. May they strengthen you to trust in him.

Charity

Through the sacraments and all the various ways God manifests his mercy, you have been given many gifts. But there are many more graces upon which you can draw as a son or daughter of God. This third virtue, charity, has incredible power to open people to God, to bring light out of darkness and hope from despair. But it can cost everything! Still, it will give more than you can imagine.

"Charity is the theological virtue by which we love God above all things for his own sake, and our neighbor as ourselves for the love of God" (*Catechism*, 1822). St. Paul described love eloquently—real love, not the Valentine's Day sentiments, but true love—whose source is God himself:

> If I speak in the tongues of men and of angels, but have not love, I am a noisy gong or a clanging cymbal. And if I have prophetic powers, and understand all mysteries and all knowledge, and if I have all faith, so as to remove mountains, but have not love, I am nothing. If I give away all I have, and if I deliver my body to be burned, but have not love, I gain nothing.
>
> Love is patient and kind; love is not jealous or boastful; it is not arrogant or rude. Love does not insist on its own way; it is not irritable or resentful; it does not rejoice at wrong, but rejoices in the right. Love bears all things, believes all things, hopes all things, endures all things.
>
> Love never ends; as for prophecies, they will pass away; as for tongues, they will cease; as for knowledge, it will pass away. For our knowledge is imperfect and our prophecy is imperfect; but when the perfect comes, the imperfect will pass away. When I was a child, I spoke like a child, I thought like a child, I reasoned like a child; when I became a man, I gave up childish ways. For now we see in a mirror dimly, but then face to face. Now I

know in part; then I shall understand fully, even as I have been fully understood. So faith, hope, love abide, these three; but the greatest of these is love. (1 Corinthians 13:1-13)

As Jesus said, "Greater love has no man than this, that a man lay down his life for his friends" (John 15:13). We don't love enough if we are afraid to defend Christ's truths in the marketplace, heedless of the embarrassment or shame it may inflict on us. We don't love if, at the first sign of conflict or lack of getting our own way, we "drop" the one we called friend or spouse. We don't yet know how much we are loved and forgiven by God if we cannot forgive another.

I learned a tremendous lesson about love when I was three years old. I woke up in the middle of the night; it was dark and quiet, so I went where most children go—to my parents' bedroom. It was empty! Frightened, I ran down the hallway of the apartment, through the dining room, to the door leading to the kitchen. There stood my mother and father with their backs to me. A man I knew was standing in the kitchen. Then I saw his wife looking fearfully at him; he had a knife in his hand. My father said, "Joe, put the knife down." Looking between my father and mother's bodies, I saw the man weeping, handing my father the knife. I saw my mother comforting his wife. No one knew I was there until things had calmed down. Joe and his wife were going through some very difficult times; he was an alcoholic trying to eke out a living in the post-Depression era. All that had produced a helplessness that drove him close to violence. But the couple got help and persevered.

Some years ago, when I was visiting my hometown, I read in the paper that this couple was celebrating their fiftieth wedding anniversary! In the midst of great turmoil, they loved one another and allowed that love to triumph. The marriage could have easily succumbed in those circumstances, but they chose not to allow it. Both of them *together* made it work. Love takes work—hard work. But if we are open to the grace of real love, we can many times triumph over the obstacles. Sometimes it is not possible, but often it is.

Love and Forgiveness

Love also involves forgiveness—again and again and again. Jesus told us to forgive "seventy times seven" (Matthew 18:22). It is the way he forgives us again and again: "Love one another as I have loved you" (John 15:12)! Hard? Yes. Seemingly impossible? Yes, by our own strength, but not with God's!

Some years ago, a young high school student and his best friend were out driving. There was an accident, and the friend was killed. The driver of the car was immediately arrested for reckless driving and put in the city jail. The next morning the father of the dead boy was seen outside the jail. News reporters were looking for a story and immediately descended upon him asking questions: "Why are you here?" "Are you going to see the driver?" "What will you say?" That father, in the midst of enormous grief, said this: "I am going to forgive him; I do not want *two* deaths on my hands." That father knew what real love meant. He knew that clinging to bitterness and unforgiveness would only lead to the poisoning of his own heart and soul and would possibly be an unbearable burden for his son's best friend.

Blessed John Paul II put it this way: "Forgiveness is the opposite of resentment and revenge, not of justice."[1] Oftentimes, when we refuse to forgive, we think we are punishing the wrongdoer, but in reality, the worst thing unforgiveness does is poison our own soul. The father who lost his son allowed the courts to handle the case; the young man would suffer the consequences of his carelessness, but that father was not going to add an intolerable burden by refusing him forgiveness. That is real love.

That power to bring Christ's love into very difficult situations, to sustain people with long-carried burdens, "to give and not to count the cost; to fight and not to heed the wound; to toil and not to seek for rest," as St. Ignatius of Loyola prayed—that power is an expression of love, but it requires us to remove ourselves and our needs at least from first place and sometimes from the equation altogether. We can do that only by the power of the Holy Spirit. That love, because it is rooted in Christ, because its source is Christ and not ourselves, has the power to turn around very serious situations.

I am encouraged by the story of Blessed Mother Teresa of Calcutta, who in 1982 asked for an hour-long cease-fire in Beirut, Lebanon, so she could evacuate thirty-seven children out of a hospital before the bombing began anew. She was told by both sides that no cease-fire was possible; it could not be done. Instead of arguing and fueling anger, she prayed, standing in the darkness, with terrorists all around her. Inexplicably, a cease-fire was called, and Mother Teresa and her sisters carried or walked all the children out to safety. When God has full authority over our minds and hearts, miracles can happen—literally!

We need, truly *need*, the power of the Holy Spirit, not just as some kind of extra, but as essential to love. God would never have asked us to love as he loves if he didn't intend to give us help to do so. And the help he gives is to share the very love between the Father and the Son—that is, the Holy Spirit—with us. Again, it is not just a holy image; it is a reality, if we are willing to turn to him in difficulty.

The concept of grace is one of Christianity's unique contributions to the flow of world history. Its impact has been felt in every culture in which the gospel has taken root. Christian author Philip Yancey recounts a poignant example of grace in post-apartheid South Africa at one of the hearings for the Truth and Reconciliation Commission, where people who had committed horrific abuses of power were offered immunity from prosecution on the condition that they confess their crimes to their victims before a tribunal.

At one hearing, a policeman named van de Broek recounted an incident when he and other officers shot an eighteen-year-old boy and burned the body, turning it on the fire like a piece of barbecue meat in order to destroy the evidence. Eight years later van de Broek returned to the same house and seized the boy's father. The wife was forced to watch as policeman bound her husband on a woodpile, poured gasoline over his body, and ignited it.

The courtroom grew hushed as the elderly woman who had lost her first son and then her husband was given a chance to respond. "What do you want from Mr. van de Broek?" the judge asked. She said she wanted van de Broek to go to the place where they burned her husband's body and gather up the dust so she could give him a decent burial. His head down, the policeman nodded in agreement.

Then she added a further request, "Mr. van de Broek took all my family away from me, and I still have a lot of love to give. Twice a month, I would like for him to come to the ghetto and spend a day with me so I can be a mother to him. And I would like Mr. van de Broek to know that he is forgiven by God, and that I forgive him too. I would like to embrace him so that he can know my forgiveness is real."

Spontaneously, some in the courtroom began singing "Amazing Grace" as the elderly woman made her way to the witness stand, but van de Broek did not hear the hymn. He had fainted, overwhelmed.[2]

Please don't settle in life by just loving those who love you. The world is in desperate need of Christians who love as Christ has loved us. Jesus died even for your enemies. He loves them and wants to give his love to them, many times through us. He wants, oftentimes, to use us to bring his wayward sons and daughters home to him. Sometimes their hearts and souls are so hardened that we think it is useless, but God never gives up; he looks for disciples who will make a way for them to reconcile with him and with others. In many cases, all we can do is offer, even when we are rejected time and time again. But most of all, we can pray, pray, pray! It is one of the most powerful expressions of our love for others.

Think Big!

Jesus gave us the image of himself as the Good Shepherd, going out to seek the poor, the lost, the blind, and the lame (John 10:1-18); often those disabilities are not just physical but mental and spiritual as well. Can you put aside your prejudices and reach out to those you encounter in your daily activities? This is the call of one who is a temple of the Holy Spirit, a disciple.

God is "in labor" even now, seeking to draw us, his sons and daughters, back to him and, in the process, to bring as many others with us as we can. And so, equipped with the gifts of our Baptism and Confirmation and with the virtues of faith, hope, and love, we can answer God's call.

Our problem is not so much that we think wrongly—though we do sometimes—but that we don't think big enough. God wants to restore and redeem and draw into union with himself our poor, weak, sinful selves. He wants to unite us with himself by the power, grace, mercy, and infinite love of his Spirit—*right now, here, today, while you are reading this book!* God wants to unite you more and more with himself by his Spirit. He desires to make you one with him and then give you the gifts you need to do his will on earth.

So in one sense, why are we surprised that God would choose, in his perfect timing, a group of college students at a small Catholic college to visit with his Holy Spirit? They simply chose to believe the Scriptures—that this was their baptismal inheritance—and they asked the Holy Spirit to come and do what they could not: "Stir up in us the gifts you gave us at Baptism and Confirmation." And he did!

Brothers and sisters in Catholic parishes throughout this country who, many years ago, opened yourselves to the gifts of the Holy Spirit through the Charismatic Renewal: let us together staunch the hemorrhaging that is going on throughout the body of Christ. Let us roll up our sleeves and sacrifice our own comfort to go out into the highways and byways to bring back the lost of our own families and the lost among the strangers in our midst. Exclude no one. Go out in the power of God's Spirit. Go out equipped with the light, strength, power, and gifts that God has given you. For one day, perhaps soon, we will have to render an account for what we have done with what we were given. Ignorance will not be accepted as an excuse. You have heard the truth for years. Get rid of your complacency. Put on the armor of God and fight! Fight for the eternal salvation of everyone you meet. God's hunger and thirst for souls will inspire and convict and challenge your own selfishness. Yield to his grace and his power, using his weapons.

All God really asks for is a confession of need—personal and corporate. He wants us to be willing to let go of everything, to be an empty vessel, ready to put down plans and hopes, to give him first place in our lives, to clearly acknowledge that we can do nothing apart from him, and then to simply be there with open hands so that God may do with us what he wills. Ask that the graces and gifts of your Baptism and Confirmation may come alive in you! He will answer; we cannot predict how. He knows you better than you know yourself; he knows us better than we know ourselves, and he will answer such a simple, wholehearted prayer. Wait upon the Lord!

CHAPTER EIGHT

"Put On the Whole Armor of God"

As disciples of Christ, we can expect to be in a battle—a battle with the enemy, who does not want us to follow Jesus or use the gifts we have received in Baptism and Confirmation to bring others to Christ. We need to be aware of this battle at all times so that we are ready to fight. The following passage from St. Paul's Letter to the Ephesians is important because it outlines the equipment that God has already given us to fight the battle effectively. Let's see what this armor consists of and how we can arm ourselves to fight the good fight of faith.

Finally, be strong in the Lord and in the strength of his might. Put on the whole armor of God, that you may be able to stand against the wiles of the devil. For we are not contending against flesh and blood, but against the principalities, against the powers, against the world rulers of this present darkness, against the spiritual hosts of wickedness in the heavenly places. Therefore take the whole armor of God, that you may be able to withstand in the evil day, and having done all, to stand. Stand therefore, having fastened the belt of truth around your wasit, and having put on the breastplate of righteousness, and having shod your feet with the equipment of the gospel of peace; besides all these, taking the shield of faith, with which you can quench all the flaming darts of the Evil One. And take the helmet of salvation, and the sword of the Spirit, which is the word of God. Pray at all times in the Spirit, with all prayer and supplication. To that end keep alert with all perseverance, making supplication for all the saints. (Ephesians 6:10-18)

St. Paul tells us to *"be strong in the Lord and in the strength of his might"* (Ephesians 6:10). That's a warning we should heed and take seriously. We can never seek the salvation of our own soul or the souls of others through our own power or strength; we will be quickly brought down. This is truly a battle with principalities and powers, and by ourselves we will be conquered. But if we trust in God at every moment, if we find our food and drink in him, we will be victorious.

The battle is formidable, and we don't stand a chance unless we are humble enough, poor enough, to receive God's instructions and be obedient to them. This goes against our pride, because we want to see ourselves as strong and self-sufficient. For example, a younger sister offers to carry something for me. I don't want to be seen as weak, so out of my mouth comes this: "Thank you, but I can handle it myself." I actually can, but how much nicer it would be to receive generously the kindness of another. But, oh no, I must prove how strong and competent I am. I don't need help!

That's a very homespun but accurate expression of pride. In one way, such an example is inconsequential, but not if it is a little expression of a much deeper independence that can work against me. If it is my independence at work, then God can offer his help and I will almost automatically try to assure him that

I can handle "this" myself, only to find that I can't—and then it will be too late! God will give us everything we need to fight the battle *if* we depend on him!

Stand Firm in Faith

We need *"the whole armor of God"* (Ephesians 6:11, 13) that he makes available to us through his Spirit so that we *"may be able to withstand in the evil day, and having done all, to stand"* (6:13). Notice that St. Paul uses the word "stand" twice in this verse and once in verse 14. Sometimes the only thing we can do is to stand. It is not a passive position, however. It is one of alertness, in which we watch over those for whom we are responsible and pray for their salvation. It means always being on duty, so to speak, always alert. It means being guardian and protector of the "gate" to my home, my heart, and the hearts, minds, and spirits of those I love. I stand, ready and available for whatever God asks.

Oftentimes, especially in our modern culture, when we find ourselves in difficult situations, we say, "If I could just *do* something!" If you *stand* in faith and *pray daily*, you are at a place in the warfare that is crucial to the outcome: the salvation of those you love. Don't ever underestimate the role of standing firm in faith and prayer. When the storms of life get too big, we tend to look for someone who can give us peace and hope. You will most often find it in the one who *stands* before God in prayer. You become a refuge for others because you have put on the armor of God!

Live Righteously

Have you *"fastened the belt of truth around you waist,"* as St. Paul instructs in Ephesians 6:14? You need to ask God for the grace to look clearly at your life. Wherever there is deceit or hypocrisy, wherever truth does not have the central place in your mind or spirit, then you need to root it out! Dig deep and pull it out by its root.

One summer while I was weeding on the grounds of our motherhouse, I came across a very beautiful green flowering plant. It actually looked kind of pretty, so I did not pull it. But the next time I looked at it, the plant was bigger, remarkably so, and so I consulted with another sister and found out that what I had thought was a new and beautiful addition to our yard was actually a very large weed! I dug it out. A few weeks later, it sprouted again, and I realized that I hadn't gotten to the bottom of the roots. I dug down a good fifteen inches before I got to the end of that root. It was sunny, hot, and humid, and it took a lot of work and perspiration to get out this one weed! So it is with us. We all have weeds—sins, past and present— that are not entirely repented of or rejected. They can even look nice on the surface, but eventually the roots of that weed can choke off life within us if we don't face them and root them out with God's grace!

This is the prelude to putting on *"the breastplate of righteousness"* (Ephesians 6:14). When we have the peace of knowing that we have repented of all past sin and are striving to eliminate the effects of that sin, we gain a confidence in God and a trust in him: *by his grace* we are living a righteous life. That is formidable armor when we are in battle. Now we are not nearly so susceptible to the lies of the devil. That is not pride because we know that the strength to recognize and repent of our sin is a grace, a gift from God. We know that we are not the source of our salvation.

Live the Gospel of Peace

"Shod your feet with the equipment of the gospel of peace" (Ephesians 6:15). God wants all men and women to know his peace—a peace that the world cannot give. In truth and humility, our brothers and sisters can come to know the Prince of Peace! You need to model God's peace for them by speaking the truth in humility, kindness, mercy, and hope.

"You keep him in perfect peace / whose mind is stayed on you / because he trusts in you" (Isaiah 26:3). This is key, brothers and sisters. Whenever you go into a situation, whether it be in the workplace, schools, parish councils, or places of civic and political responsibility, you need to be united to the Lord in prayer first. That means that you have brought to him everything you know about the situation. You have talked to God about your anger or fear, your jealousy or desire for revenge—whatever relates to the circumstances. You have commended the discussion and the outcome to him. You have asked him to show you the part *he* wants you to play—not necessarily the part you want to play. Ask him! The Lord can be very practical. Sometimes he gives us the answer to our question or the words he wants us to say before we go to the event or meeting—sometimes right at the moment. Trust him! He will cover you with his peace, for you are in the center of his will. Let your strongest desire be not to win the argument but to make room in the discussion for the Prince of Peace to be present.

"Besides all these, taking the shield of faith, with which you can quench all the flaming darts of the Evil One" (Ephesians 6:16). When you are attacked for what you say, ask the Holy Spirit for help. Answer out of your faith. Don't attack in response, no matter how much you are attacked. Speak the truth again and again. Rely on the truth of what you say. Let the Spirit of God have authority over your mind and spirit so that no attack will disturb your peace and hope. Seek constantly to grow in understanding your faith and, even more, to know and love more deeply the Author of your faith!

Many years ago, a good friend of mine was standing at a pro-life demonstration. Lines were drawn as the opposing side faced the demonstrators. The media loved it, and my friend wanted very much to get into the fray, since she is very articulate. But instead, because of inspiration from God, she left the area and went to a nearby store, purchasing coffee and doughnuts for as many as she could. She returned, found her way back to her place, and began handing out the doughnuts and coffee. A quiet fell, there was a collective sigh of relief, and then the media began asking some good questions, to which she was able to respond. No, the war wasn't won that day, but her generosity allowed for a moment of calm. She had prayed, believing that God was with her, and asked God what to do. That's an action based on faith, and the Spirit of God blessed her action.

The enemy cannot flourish in a climate of peace, hope, and reasonable discussion. But he will thrive when we give in to anger, bitterness, personal attacks, or even violence (even in the name of being "pro-life"). Don't let the enemy pull you to his side, even by understandable anger and indignation. There is a place to express your anger, but pro-life rallies may be a better place to evangelize than to attack. This is obviously only one kind of situation in which we need to hold up the shield of faith against the fiery darts, but you can apply the principles here to other situations that need the strength of faith.

We need to trust God! By prayer and preparation, let him direct your arguments, your advocacy for an issue, or your challenges in a relationship or job. When he guards and guides you through your submission, you will know a peace that the world cannot give. There is an underlying peace that no external circumstance can take away, and those who hear will receive more purely what God wants his people to know. It may not be what you intended to say, but the fruits of obedience are a peace and confidence that will be imparted to those to whom you speak.

Live in the Truth

"Take the helmet of salvation" (Ephesians 6:17). The helmet of salvation is the truth. Put on this helmet and cover yourself with the truth that God has created you—uniquely! He loves you so much that he gave his only begotten Son to die on a cross for you so that you could be united with him, now and in eternity. Know the truth that you cannot save yourself. Yield to God, his plan, and his way, and you will know peace and happiness even in this vale of tears. You are in truth his son, his daughter. Live out your inheritance.

Let these truths penetrate deeply within you until they inform your thoughts, words, and actions. Memorize Scripture, especially those passages that deal with the battleground of the mind. You have to play your part in training your mind to hunger for the truth, to latch onto it when you hear it, and to cling to it tightly. Let that truth protect your mind; it will guard you from the insidious lies of the enemy—lies such as "I am stupid," "I am worthless," "I am dumb," or "I can't do anything right." You know the kinds of thoughts that can come into your head. If you really put on the "helmet of salvation," you will be able to dismiss such lies, and someday you'll be able to laugh at them, even in the midst of battle.

We are also to take *the sword of the Spirit, which is the word of God*" (Ephesians 6:17). In other parts of this book, I have referred to the power of God's word to impart wisdom, truth, peace, and hope that the world cannot give. This word is "living and active, sharper than any two-edged sword," with the power to separate bone from marrow (Hebrews 4:12). It can change you if you read it and heed it. Please let the word of God have a daily place in your life and prayer. This is essential!

Persist in Prayer

"*Pray at all times in the Spirit, with all prayer and supplication*" (Ephesians 6:18). Scripture tells us that Jesus lives forever to make intercession for us (Hebrews 7:25). When we pray the prayers of the Mass and the Divine Office, our prayer is most often offered "through Christ our Lord." Why? Because Jesus is praying before the Father—always—on our behalf. When we pray, we are to unite our prayer with Jesus before the throne of the Father. We are never alone when we pray. Know that, and be confident that God hears your prayer.

Always, God wants repentance, a turning to him, a reliance on him, an inclusion of him in our own life's plans. So many young people today exclude God from their lives, sometimes by omission, sometimes by purposefully rejecting God's presence. Not only young people, but all of us are guilty of these things at times. So when we pray for spouses, children, relatives, and friends, always pray first that each comes to know, love, and serve God. Put first in your prayer what is first in God's heart, and you will be amazed at what happens.

Finally, St. Paul tells us to *"keep alert with all persever-ance, making supplication for all the saints"* (Ephesians 6:18). Perseverance is not easy, especially when we don't see an answer to our prayers coming quickly! To persevere in prayer, to never give up praying for what our children and other family mem-bers need, takes courage and faith, but God will not disappoint.

Let me share with you a story that has encouraged me. A young man in a very large city was a heroin addict. One day about a year ago, he said to himself, "I need to go to church." He had not been in a church in years, and he did not even know where one was. His brain was deeply affected by the drugs, and he could not even think clearly about the simplest things. But this thought would not leave his mind. Then he remembered that his great-grandmother had gone to a church in that same city. He went in search of it, and on a Sunday morning, he went to the service. A minister was asking people who wanted Jesus in their hearts to come down the aisle for prayer. This young man stumbled down the aisle and told the minister he needed prayer. The minister asked his name. When the young man told him, the minister jumped back in surprise. "*You* are Joe Smith?" the minister asked. "Yes," the young man replied. The minister then spoke to the whole congregation, telling them that here was Joe Smith! The people began to cry, shout, and laugh.

This poor young man was bewildered. How did these people know him? Then the minister explained, "Many years ago, your great-grandmother asked us to pray for you. Every Sunday since then, we have prayed in faith for you, and now here you are!" Such an experience has the power to set this young man on a new path; we shall see. But for now, look at God's faithfulness to persistent prayer over many years. Never give up praying for those you love. Pray most of all that they will come to know, love, and serve the God who has created them and then saved them for eternal life.

"Put on the whole armor of God!" He has made this equipment available to us so that we might endure and conquer in this battle of earthly life. Through it he imparts his grace, his power, and his very presence.

CHAPTER NINE

A Call to Repentance

As the years go by, I become more and more awed by the gifts that God has given to so many of us all over the world. He gave them to teach, to strengthen, to heal, and to equip us for the building up of the body of Christ. Why did he visit us so clearly in this time period (1967 to the present day) in which you and I are living out our lives? We know what is happening to the faith of Western Europeans and North Americans. All over the world, the same trends will be seen in the months and years ahead, especially because of the import of secular Western culture in places around the globe. As Pope Benedict told us, a tsunami of secularism is beginning to engulf the world. Tsunamis destroy—they wipe out. Yes, God is merciful, *but* when he gives us gifts to be able to face the challenges and then we simply take them for ourselves or ignore or discard their God-given purposes, we run the very real risk of having to face his judgment!

We are part of the family of God, brothers and sisters of the Lord Jesus. What I do or don't do affects the human family in which I live, but it also affects—sometimes deeply—my family in Christ. On the day of judgment, I will need to render an account of what I have done with the graces of the sacraments I have received—Baptism, Confirmation, Reconciliation, the Eucharist, and Marriage or Holy Orders. In addition, because the gifts of the Holy Spirit found in Isaiah 11:2-3 were given to me to form me and mature me into the very image and likeness of my Creator and Father and Redeemer, I will be asked what I have done with all the grace that was poured out on me. Have I grown over the years to resemble my Father and my Savior more and more? Of course, we cannot do this on our own, but the grace is given; our call is to cooperate. Have we?

Other gifts listed in 1 Corinthians 12, 13, and 14 were given, in part, to empower us to contribute to the forming and empowering of new sons and daughters, sisters and brothers, to be channels of the grace and mercy of God to all, especially to those who walk in darkness. "No man is an island," the English poet John Milton famously said. But our culture has worked against God's plan so that many people today do not know who they are, where they came from, or where they are going. We are part of the problem if we are not helping our brothers and sisters with the gifts we each have been given. As God fashions and uses us according to his will, we must help them to draw closer to their Savior, to know the love of their Father in heaven, and to experience the power of the Holy Spirit.

It is my belief that we—all of us, each of us—have much we need to repent of!

We need to repent for treating the gifts of the Holy Spirit as a kind of personal possession, to be used when and where and how we think fit. We are stewards, not owners, and stewards must always give an account for how they have used the Master's gifts.

We need to repent for jealousy and envy regarding the gifts of others and their use. When I give in to these temptations, I am harming the body I am part of—the body of Christ.

We need to repent for using gifts of worship and praise only as long as they fit into our personal desires, and for attending prayer meetings only when we "felt like it." Maybe we would go only if a certain person was leading or giving the talk. In other words, we would participate when the prayer meeting met *our* perceived needs or desires.

We need to repent for the prayer meetings that "died" because of division and dislike, envy and strife, calumny, and even hatred! In some ways, the enemy succeeded in disbanding the family that God was empowering us to be part of, where we could grow together as members of God's family, genuine brothers and sisters in Christ. Do I need to repent for the part I played in the dwindling or elimination of prayer groups in my parish, my diocese, or my region? Did I ever think about the person who might have found Christ if there were still a prayer meeting in my parish? What does God want me to do?

God's plan was to form and equip an army of radical disciples, thoroughly in love with him and willing to serve him, to bring his presence by his Spirit into a world that was scattered and fragmented and dispirited—and the world today, in many ways, is even more scattered and fragmented and dispirited. Again and again, in our nation and in many parts of the world, we continue to reject his presence from our private and public life.

BUT, even now, in the darkness of our selfishness and sin, God's word gives us hope: "The steadfast love of the LORD never ceases, / his mercies never come to an end; / they are new every morning;

/ great is your faithfulness. / 'The LORD is my portion,' says my soul, / 'therefore I will hope in him'" (Lamentations 3:22-24).

I say all of this because I believe the Charismatic Renewal as a whole in the U.S.—and each of us as individuals—needs to repent wherever we have personally failed or were part of some corporate failure.

We also need to engage in a solemn act of repentance that is not simply the recitation of a prayer of repentance but a time to ask God to show us how we have failed him and to ask forgiveness for how we have misused or not used the gifts we have been given—individually and corporately.

We need to humble ourselves before him and ask for a second chance. The gifts are in us, but we need to consecrate them for his glory, not our own. We need to put him and his will dead center in our lives, pleading with him for the grace to carry out his will. We need to cry out for the Holy Spirit to fall upon us again. The grace is in us by Baptism and Confirmation, yes, but we need to put our faith and our will behind the truth that God wants a strong family of sons and daughters who will, in the power of the Holy Spirit, defend and protect and respect his presence within each of us. Then his light will genuinely shine out through our personalities, our gifts, and all the various roles we may be asked to play. This is not a plan we can concoct. It will be his plan that we accept, as humble servants, sons and daughters of a God who loves us and does not want to see anyone of his family perish.

Come, Holy Spirit, I welcome you into my life. May our Lord and Savior have mercy upon me and upon us together! May our Father raise us to new life in you. May he, in mercy, give new life to our bodies and spirits. Open us, Holy Spirit, to the work of evangelism that you want to accomplish right where each of us lives. Help us so that you might be more and more, each day, the center of our thoughts, our words, and our actions. Give us grace to forget ourselves, to help one another, pray for one another, and carry one another, until we all stand before your judgment seat, able to render an account freely and even joyfully of our lives spent in carrying out your will!

Age does not matter. Whether we are sixteen or sixty, eight or eighty, ninety or one hundred, weak or strong, healthy or ill, all of us have a part to play in surrendering our wills once again, or for the first time, that God may use us for his beloved body, the Church, for our nation, and for the salvation of the lost everywhere across the world.

If my people who are called by my name humble themselves, and pray and seek my face, and turn from their wicked ways, then I will hear from heaven, and will forgive their sin and heal their land. (2 Chronicles 7:14)

And [Jesus] answered them, "Do you think that these Galileans were worse sinners than all the other Galileans, because they suffered thus? I tell you, No; but unless you repent you will all likewise perish. Or those eighteen upon whom the Tower in Silo'am fell and killed them, do you think that they were worse offenders than all the others who dwelt in Jerusalem? I tell you, No; but unless you repent you will all likewise perish." (Luke 13:2-5)

See that you do not refuse him who is speaking. For if they did not escape when they refused him who warned them on earth, much less shall we escape if we reject him who warns from heaven. His voice then shook the earth; but now he has promised, "Yet once more I will shake not only the earth but also the heaven." This phrase, "Yet once more," indicates the removal of what is shaken, as of what has been made, in order that what cannot be shaken may remain. Therefore let us be grateful for receiving a kingdom that cannot be shaken, and thus let us offer to God acceptable worship, with reverence and awe; for our God is a consuming fire. (Hebrews 12:25-29)

While American author and clergyman Edward Everett Hale does not sit in the same company as Scripture, nevertheless, from a human perspective, he hit the proverbial nail on the head when he said the following words. We can use his words as the response we need to make, given our spiritual condition today: "I am only one, but I am one. I cannot do everything, but I can do something. What I can do, I ought to do, and by the grace of God, I will do."

Conclusion

In him, according to the purpose of him who accomplishes all things according to the counsel of his will, we who first hoped in Christ have been destined and appointed to live for the praise of his glory. In him you also, who have heard the word of truth, the gospel of your salvation, and have believed in him, were sealed with the promised Holy Spirit, who is the guarantee of our inheritance until we acquire possession of it, to the praise of his glory.

—Ephesians 1:11-14

I began this little book with an analogy about our physical need to drink from good, clean water or risk the possibility of illness or even death. I beg you, drink from the life-giving waters that flowed from the side of the Savior who died for you. I have tried to show you some of the ways to that Source; these waters are cleansing and healing, but they need to be drunk daily. The waters are life-giving, not only for a time, but for eternity!

Now I will end this book with another analogy that I hope will help you as much as it has helped me. When I taught at Franciscan University in Steubenville, Ohio, there was, one afternoon, a sudden windstorm that packed a powerful punch. I was on campus at the time, but later, when the all-clear signals were given and we could return home, I was shocked to see the damage from such a brief though intense storm. Our residential area was a seven- or eight-block street that was lined with tall beautiful trees that formed a canopy over the area. In the summer the sunlight through those large leafy trees was just lovely. This day I stared at seven blocks of trees, a number of them downed, uprooted, and damaged beyond repair. I couldn't believe it; the roots of those large trees were *very* shallow. I thought I had learned a lesson spiritually about the need to put down deep roots in Christ in order to withstand the storms of life, and I used that example in many talks.

However, last fall I was speaking at a diocesan conference in the Midwest, and I used this example to explain that if we are going to participate in the New Evangelization, we need to make sure our roots are deep in Christ. In the New Evangelization, it is not primarily a matter of teaching people Church doctrine but, rather, of showing forth in our lives the presence of Christ so that those who hear the good news would be drawn to him. If our roots are not deep in Christ, if we don't know him, what do we have to offer?

After my talk, a man came up and asked me if I knew why the roots of those trees were so shallow. I said I presumed it was related to the kind of trees they were, which I could not identify. "No," he said. "The problem was that the roots were never tested." He then went on to explain that water must have been plentiful for those trees; the roots did not have to dig down deep to find water. As a result, although they looked beautiful and strong, they were, in reality, very weak.

As a people, we have not really been tested. We have not had to search deeply for strength, wisdom, and courage when it comes to matters of faith. We have enjoyed peace and the freedom to worship, to speak, to evangelize, to invite, to form Bible study groups and prayer groups, and to hold retreats and conferences, with no penalties attached to doing so.

That could change. If we don't let our roots go down deep into Christ, we will not survive the storms. It is as simple as that. And if we cannot survive, what will happen to the faith of our children, our grandchildren, and those yet unborn? As this man shared with me his understanding of how roots are formed, I was reminded of a story that Andrew Murray, a Dutch Protestant preacher from South Africa, recounted in one of his little books on intercession.[1]

He related a story about this marvelous grapevine in England, which he saw in the late 1800s. Depending on the type of grape, a grapevine usually produces thirty to eighty clusters of grapes in a season. This particular vine was yielding hundreds of clusters in each season. The root system was tapped to discover why this vine was so abundant, and it was found that the roots had traveled over one mile into the luxurious muck of the Thames River! During famine and war, it had not only survived but flourished.

And it still does! Some ten years ago, some friends of mine were visiting England. I asked them if they could find out what happened to that vine. (Remember, Andrew Murray was relating his experience from the late 1800s.) They found it, and in the first decades of the twenty-first century, that vine is still producing a great harvest! They even took photos to show me. Generation upon generation is still reaping the abundant fruit from one vine that put its roots down deep and labored until it was rooted in a source of life that continues to nourish it to this day.

My brothers and sisters, God has lavished his gifts upon us. The fruits of Christ given through Baptism and Confirmation are available to us for the asking. Let us undertake the task of digging deep, whatever it costs, until we drink from the life-giving water that flows from the side of Christ. Let our roots be established in him. Don't settle for any other source of water, no matter how tempting.

God Will Use You

For those of us who were or are part of the Charismatic Renewal, there is a need for a season of repentance. We have been given so much, and when I write something like this, I realize even more the inestimable treasure that we have received, particularly in the Sacraments of Baptism, Confirmation, the Eucharist, and Reconciliation. We are the people of God. Let us ask God for forgiveness for the times we have not used or have misused all the graces he has placed at our disposal. Let us repent of our indifference and complacency and return to the Lord with fasting, weeping, and mourning. In a way, this is a call to all Christians everywhere in the world. If we do so with humility and a true willingness to change, God may grant us mercy.

Over and over, I ask myself this question: Why did God pour out his Holy Spirit in such a lavish way in our lifetime? Why?

He saw many people rejecting him.

He saw the proliferation of false gods: money, sex, and power.

He saw wars and rumors of wars.

He saw the rise in cohabitation, rejection of marriage, absentee fathers, and opposition to authority.

He saw so many losing their lives by searching for happiness in drugs, alcohol, and sex.

He saw the scourge of abortion growing by leaps and bounds.

And as only God can, he saw what awaited us in the decades to come and knew that we didn't stand a chance without his direct intervention.

He came because we asked specifically for help through Blessed Pope John XXIII. When God's people are willing to admit their weakness, sin, and need, he will respond. He will come and save us. He is the Good Shepherd. Our Shepherd wants us to ask for his help, help that we cannot manufacture or produce. We do not even know how deep our need is. We have become a people who are so self-sufficient that we look only to ourselves and to what science and technology provide. As a people, we are unprepared to fight the battle of principalities and powers. We cannot fight the spiritual forces that wage war on our souls and families, our Church, and our countries, without the significant intervention of God.

"If you love me, you will keep my commandments. And I will ask the Father, and he will give you another Counselor, to be with you for ever, even the Spirit of truth, whom the world cannot receive, because it neither sees him nor knows him; you know him, for he dwells with you, and will be in you" (John 14:15-17).

As I have said, the Holy Spirit *is* the love between the Father and the Son, a love so great that it is beyond our capacity to understand, a limitless love that "generates" the third Person of the Blessed Trinity. That love is given to you; it is poured out on you in Baptism, washing over you and through you and in you until you become a child of God—a living temple of the most high God, a true son or daughter of God. That is who you are! Why would God not respond when his servants cry out for help in and with and through Jesus?

The New Evangelization can only be successful if there is a "new Pentecost" in our hearts, a new commitment to serve him as he deserves to be served. Pentecost preceded the first evangelization. God will give us and equip us with all that we need, *but* right now we have to be drinking daily, even hourly, from the springs of salvation. Give God time. Lay your soul bare before him. Be reconciled with God and others where you need to be. But most of all, spend time with God. Learn to know him; let him know you. Then he will reveal himself more to you, often in the ordinary events of life. If you are attuned to him, as we always are to those we love, God will reveal himself to you and use you for the rebuilding of his kingdom in our day.

For this reason, because I have heard of your faith in the Lord Jesus and your love toward all the saints, I do not cease to give thanks for you, remembering you in my prayers, that the God of our Lord Jesus Christ, the Father of glory, may give you a spirit of wisdom and of revelation in the knowledge of him, having the eyes of your hearts enlightened, that you may know what is the hope to which he has called you, what are the riches of his glorious inheritance in the saints, and what is the immeasurable greatness of his power in us who believe, according to the working of his great might which he accomplished in Christ when he raised him from the dead and made him sit at his right hand in the heavenly places, far above all rule and authority and power and dominion, and above every name that is named, not only in this age but also in that which is to come; and he has put all things under his feet and has made him the head over all things for the Church, which is his body, the fullness of him who fills all in all.

And you he made alive, when you were dead through the trespasses and sins in which you once walked. . . . But God, who is rich in mercy, out of the great love with which he loved us, even when we were dead through our trespasses, made us alive together with Christ (by grace you have been saved), and raised us up with him, and made us sit with him in the heavenly places in Christ Jesus, that in the coming ages he might show the immeasurable riches of his grace in kindness toward us in Christ Jesus. For by grace you have been saved through faith; and this is not your own doing, it is the gift of God. (Ephesians 1:15–2:2, 4-8)

Baptism in the Holy Spirit

General Audience of Pope John Paul II
September 6, 1989

When the Church, originating in the sacrifice of the cross, began her early journey by means of the descent of the Holy Spirit in the upper room at Pentecost, "her time" began. "It was the time of the Church" as collaborator of the Spirit in the mission of making the redemption by Christ fruitful among humanity from generation to generation. In this mission and in collaboration with the Spirit, the Church realizes the sacramentality which the Second Vatican Council attributes to her when it teaches: "The Church is in Christ like a sacrament or as a sign and instrument both of a very closely knit union with God and of the unity of the whole human race" (*Lumen Gentium*, 1). This sacramentality has a deep significance in relation to the mystery of Pentecost, which gives the Church the strength and the charisms to work visibly among the whole human family.

In this catechesis we wish to consider principally the relationship between Pentecost and the sacrament of Baptism. We know that the coming of the Holy Spirit had been announced at the Jordan together with the coming of Christ. John the Baptist was to link the two comings, and indeed to show their intimate connection when speaking of baptism: "He will baptize you with the Holy Spirit" (Mark 1:8). "He will baptize you with the Holy Spirit and with fire" (Matthew 3:11). This link between the Holy Spirit and fire is found in the context of biblical language, which already in the Old Testament showed fire as the means adopted by God to purify consciences (cf. Isaiah 1:25; 6:5-7; Zechariah 13:9; Malachi 3:2-3; Sirach 2:5, etc.). In its turn, the baptism practiced in Judaism and in other ancient religious was a ritual immersion, which signified a regenerating purification. John the Baptist had adopted this practice of baptizing with water, while emphasizing that its value was not merely ritual but oral, because it was "for conversion" (cf. Matthew 3:2, 6, 8, 11; Luke 3:10-14). Besides, it was a kind of initiation through which those who received it became the Baptist's disciples and formed around him a community characterized by its eschatological expectation of the Messiah (cf. Matthew 3:2, 11; John 1:13-14). Nevertheless, it was a baptism with water. It therefore did not have the power of sacramental purification. Such power would have been characteristic of the baptism of fire "in itself an element much more powerful than water" brought by the Messiah. John proclaimed the preparatory and symbolic function of his baptism in relation to the Messiah, who was to baptize "with the Holy Spirit and with fire" (Matthew 3:11; cf. 3, 7, 10, 12; John 1:33). He added that the Messiah would thoroughly purify with the fire of the Spirit those who were well disposed, gathered like "wheat in the granary." Yet he would burn "the chaff . . . with unquenchable fire" (Matthew 3:12), like the "hell of fire" (cf. Matthew 18:8-9), a symbol of the end destined for all who did not let themselves be purified (cf. Isaiah 66:24; Judith 16:17; Sirach 7:17; Zephaniah 1:18; Psalm 21:10, etc.).

While developing his role as prophet and precursor along the lines of Old Testament symbolism, the Baptist one day met Jesus by the Jordan. He recognized him as the Messiah, proclaimed that he is "the Lamb of God, who takes away the sin of the world" (John 1:29), and baptized him at his request (cf. Matthew 3:14-15). Yet at the same time he testified to the messiahship of Jesus, whose mere announcer and precursor he claimed to be. This testimony of John was supplemented by his own statement to his disciples and hearers concerning the experience which he had on that occasion, and which perhaps had reminded him of the Genesis narrative about the end of the flood (cf. Genesis 8:10): "I saw the Spirit descend as a dove from heaven, and it remained on him. I myself did not know him, but he who sent me to baptize with water said to me: 'He on whom you see the Spirit descend and remain, this is he who baptizes with the Holy Spirit . . . '" (John 1:32-33; cf. Matthew 3:16; Mark 1:8; Luke 3:22).

"Baptizing in the Holy Spirit" means regenerating humanity with the power of God's Spirit. That is what the Messiah does. As Isaiah had foretold (11:2; 42:1), the Spirit rests on him, filling his humanity with divine strength, from his Incarnation to the fullness of the resurrection after his death on the cross (cf. John 7:29; 14:26; 16:7, 8; 20:22; Luke 24:49). Having acquired this fullness, Jesus the Messiah can give the new baptism in the Spirit of whom he is full (cf. John 1:33; Acts 1:5). From his glorified humanity, as from a fountain of living water, the Spirit will flow over the world (cf. John 7:37-39; 19:34; cf. Romans 5:5). This is the announcement which the Baptist made when bearing witness to Christ on the occasion of his baptism, in which are found the symbols of water and fire, expressing the mystery of the new life-giving energy which the Messiah and the Spirit have poured out on the world.

During his ministry, Jesus also spoke of his passion and death as a baptism which he himself must receive: a baptism, because he must be totally immersed in the suffering symbolized by the cup which he must drink (cf. Mark 10:38; 14:36). But it was a baptism which Jesus connected to the other symbol of fire. In this it is easy enough to glimpse the Spirit who "pours out" his humanity, and who one day, after the fire of the cross, would flow over the world. He would spread the baptism of fire which Jesus so longed to receive that he was in anguish until it was accomplished in him (cf. Luke 12:50).

In the encyclical *Dominum et Vivificantem* I wrote: "The Old Testament on several occasions speaks of fire from heaven which burnt the oblations presented by men. By analogy one can say that the Holy Spirit is the fire from heaven which works in the depths of the mystery of the cross. The Holy Spirit as Love and Gift comes down, in a certain sense, into the very heart of the sacrifice which is offered on the cross. Referring here to the biblical tradition we can say: he consumes this sacrifice with the fire of the love which united the Son with the Father in the trinitarian communion. And since the sacrifice of the cross is an act proper to Christ, also in this sacrifice he receives the Holy Spirit. He receives the Holy Spirit in such a way that afterward 'and he alone with God the Father' can give him to the apostles, to the Church, to humanity. He alone sends the Spirit from the Father. He alone appears to the apostles in the upper room, breathes on them and says: 'Receive the Holy Spirit; if you forgive the sins of any, they are forgiven' (cf. John 20:23)" (n. 41).

Thus John's messianic announcement at the Jordan is fulfilled: "He will baptize you with the Holy Spirit and with fire" (Matthew 3:11; cf. Luke 3:16). Here also is found the realization of the symbolism by which God himself is shown as a column of fire which guides the people through the desert (cf. Exodus 13:21-22); as the word of fire through which "the mountain (Sinai) burned with fire to the heart of heaven" (Deuteronomy 4:11); as a fire of ardent glory with love for Israel (cf. Deuteronomy 4:24). What Christ himself promised when he said that he had come to cast fire on the earth (cf. Luke 12:49) is fulfilled, while the Book of Revelation would say of him that his eyes are blazing like a fire (cf. Revelation 1:14; 2:18; 19:12). Thus it is clear that the Holy Spirit is represented by the fire (cf. Acts 2:3). All this happens in the paschal mystery, when Christ "received the baptism with which he himself was to be baptized" (cf. Mark 10:38) in the sacrifice on the cross, and in the mystery of Pentecost, when the risen and glorified Christ pours his Spirit on the apostles and on the Church.

According to St. Paul, by that "baptism of fire" received in his sacrifice, Christ in his resurrection became the "last Adam," "a life-giving spirit" (cf. 1 Corinthians 15:45). For this reason the risen Christ announced to the apostles: "John baptized with water but before many days you shall be baptized with the Holy Spirit" (Acts 1:5). By the work of the "last Adam," Christ, "the life-giving Spirit" (cf. John 6:83) would be given to the apostles and to the Church.

On Pentecost Day this baptism is revealed. It is the new and final baptism which purifies and sanctifies through a new life. It is the baptism in virtue of which the Church is born in the eschatological perspective which extends "to the close of the age" (cf. Matthew 28:20); not merely the Church of Jerusalem of the apostles and the Lord's immediate disciples, but the entire Church, taken in her universality, realized through the times and in the places where she is established on earth.

The tongues of fire which accompanied the Pentecost event in the upper room at Jerusalem are the sign of that fire which Jesus Christ brought and enkindled on earth (cf. Luke 12:43): the fire of the Holy Spirit.

In the light of Pentecost we can also understand better the significance of Baptism as a first sacrament, insofar as it is a work of the Holy Spirit. Jesus himself had referred to it in his conversation with Nicodemus: "Truly, truly, I say to you, unless one is born of water and the Spirit, he cannot enter the kingdom of God" (John 3:5). In this same conversation Jesus referred also to his future death on the cross (cf. John 3:14-15) and to his heavenly glory (cf. John 3:13). It is the baptism of the sacrifice, from which the baptism by water, the first sacrament of the Church, received power to effect her birth from the Holy Spirit and to open to humanity the "entrance to God's kingdom." Indeed, as St. Paul writes to the Romans, "Do you not know that all of us who have been baptized into Christ were baptized into his death? We are buried therefore with him by baptism into death, so that as Christ was raised from the dead by the glory of the Father, we too might walk in newness of life" (Romans 6:3-4). This baptismal walk in newness of life began on Pentecost day at Jerusalem.

Several times in his letters the Apostle points out the significance of Baptism (cf. 1 Corinthians 6:11; Titus 3:5; 2 Corinthians

1:22; Ephesians 1:13). He sees it as a "washing of regeneration and renewal in the Holy Spirit" (Titus 3:5); a portent of justification "in the name of the Lord Jesus Christ" (1 Corinthians 6:11; cf. 2 Corinthians 1:22); as a "seal of the promised Holy Spirit" (cf. Ephesians 1:13); as "a guarantee of the Spirit in our hearts" (cf. 2 Corinthians 1:22). Given this presence of the Holy Spirit in the baptized, the Apostle recommends to the Christians of that time and also repeats to us today: "Do not grieve the Holy Spirit of God, in whom you were sealed for the day of redemption" (Ephesians 4:30).[1]

Regina Caeli

Pope Benedict XVI

May 11, 2008

Dear Brothers and Sisters,

Today we are celebrating the Solemnity of Pentecost, an ancient Jewish feast on which the Covenant that God made with his People on Mount Sinai (cf. Exodus 19) was commemorated. It also became a Christian feast because of what happened on that day fifty days after Jesus' Pasch. We read in the Acts of the Apostles that the disciples were praying all together in the Upper Room when the Holy Spirit descended upon them powerfully, as wind and as fire. They then began to proclaim in many tongues the Good News of Christ's Resurrection (cf. 2:1-4). This was the "Baptism of the Holy Spirit" which had been foretold by John the Baptist: "I baptize you with water," he said to the crowds, "but he who is coming after me is mightier than I . . . ; he will baptize you with the Holy Spirit and with fire" (Matthew 3:11). In fact, Jesus' entire mission aimed at giving the Spirit of God to men and women and at baptizing them in his regenerative "bath." This was brought about with his glorification (cf. John 7:39), that is, through his death and Resurrection: then the Spirit of God was poured out in superabundance, like a cascade capable of purifying every heart, extinguishing the fire of evil and kindling the flame of divine love in the world.

The Acts of the Apostles present Pentecost as the fulfillment of this promise and hence as the culmination of Jesus' entire mission. After his Resurrection, he himself ordered the disciples to stay in Jerusalem, because, he said, "before many days you shall be baptized with the Holy Spirit" (Acts 1:5); and he added: "You shall receive power when the Holy Spirit has come upon you; and you shall be my witnesses in Jerusalem and in all Judea and Samaria and to the end of the earth" (1:8). Thus Pentecost is in a special way the Baptism of the Church which carries out her universal mission starting from the roads of Jerusalem with the miraculous preaching in humanity's different tongues. In this Baptism of the Holy Spirit the personal and community dimension, the "I" of the disciple and the "we" of the Church, are inseparable. The Holy Spirit consecrates the person and at the same time makes him or her a living member of the Mystical Body of Christ, sharing in the mission of witnessing to his love. And this takes place through the Sacraments of Christian initiation: Baptism and Confirmation. In my Message for the next World Youth Day 2008, I have proposed to the young people that they rediscover the Holy Spirit's presence in their lives and thus the importance of these Sacraments. Today I would like to extend the invitation to all: let us rediscover, dear brothers and sisters, the beauty of being baptized in the Holy Spirit; let us recover awareness of our Baptism and our Confirmation, ever timely sources of grace.

Let us ask the Virgin Mary to obtain also today a renewed Pentecost for the Church that will imbue in all, and especially in the young, the joy of living and witnessing to the Gospel.[2]

Bibliography

Benedict XVI. *The Fathers*. San Francisco: Our Sunday Visitor, 2008.

Burrows, Ruth, OCD. *Essence of Prayer*. Mahwah, NJ: HiddenSpring, 2006.

Dajczer, Tadeusz. *The Gift of Faith*. Fort Collins, CO: In the Arms of Mary Foundation, 2000.

John Paul II. *Novo Millennio Ineunte* (At the Beginning of a New Millenium). Boston: Pauline Books and Media, 2001.

————. *Vita Consecrata* (The Consecrated Life). Boston: Pauline Books and Media, 1996.

Leiva-Merikakis, Erasmo. *The Way of the Disciple*. San Francisco: Ignatius Press, 2003.

Martin, Ralph. *Will Many Be Saved? What Vatican II Actually Teaches and Its Implications for the New Evangelization*. Grand Rapids, MI: William B. Eerdmans Publishing Company, 2012.

Ratzinger, Cardinal Joseph. *Gospel, Catechesis, Catechism: Sidelights on the Catechism of the Catholic Church*. San Francisco: Ignatius Press, 1997.

Endnotes

Introduction

1. John Paul II, Encyclical *Redemptoris Missio* [Mission of the Redeemer], issued December 7, 1990, http://www .vatican.va/holy_father/john_paul_ii/encyclicals/documents/ hf_jp-ii_enc_07121990_redemptoris-missio_en.html.

2. Benedict XVI, *New Outpourings of the Holy Spirit,* trans. Michael Miller and Henry Taylor (San Francisco: Ignatius Press, 2007), 115.

Chapter One: Come, Holy Spirit!

1. Apostolic Constitution, *Humanae Salutis*, with which Pope John XXIII convoked the Second Vatican Council, December 25, 1961. English translation accessed at http://jakomonchak .files.wordpress.com/2011/12/humanae-salutis.pdf. This can be accessed in Latin on the Vatican website at http://www.vatican .va/holy_father/john_xxiii/apost_constitutions/documents/ hf_j-xxiii_apc_19611225_humanae-salutis_po.html.

Chapter Two: Where Are We Now?

1. Paul VI, Homily on the Feast of Sts. Peter and Paul, June 29, 1972, http://www.vatican.va/holy_father/paul_vi/homilies/1972/ documents/hf_p-vi_hom_19720629_it.html.

2. "Prophecies Given at St. Peter's Basilica during the Closing Eucharist on Pentecost Monday," *New Covenant Magazine* 5 (July 1975): 26.

3. Ibid.

4. Ralph Martin, *Will Many Be Saved? What Vatican II Actually Teaches and Its Implications for the New Evangelization* (Grand Rapids, MI: William Eerdmans Company, 2012), 284.

5. Ralph Martin, *The Urgency of the New Evangelization* (Huntington, IN: Our Sunday Visitor, 2013).

6. John Paul II, "Holy Father's Speech for the World Congress of Ecclesial Movements and New Communities," May 27, 1998, 4, 5, http://www.vatican .va/roman_curia/pontifical_councils/laity/documents/ rc_pc_laity_doc_27051998_movements-speech-hf_en.html.

7. Benedict XVI, Regina Caeli, May 11, 2008, http://www .vatican.va/holy_father/benedict_xvi/angelus/2008/documents/ hf_ben-xvi_reg_20080511_pentecoste_en.html.

Chapter Three: The Call to Discipleship

1. Erasmo Leiva-Merikakis, *The Way of the Disciple* (San Francisco: Ignatius Press, 2003), 12.

2. Ruth Burrows, OCD, *Essence of Prayer* (Mahwah, NJ: HiddenSpring, 2006), 21.

3. Ibid., 78.

Chapter Four: Keep the Fire Burning

1. Augustine, *Exposition of the Psalms, Volume 3*, trans. Maria Boulding, OSB (New York City: New City Press, 2004), 306.

2. John Paul II, Apostolic Letter *Novo Millennio Ineunte* [At the Beginning of the New Millenium], issued January 6, 2001, 16–28, http://www.vatican.va/ holy_father/john_paul_ii/apost_letters/documents/ hf_jp-ii_apl_20010106_novo-millennio-ineunte_en.html.

3. Ibid., 33.

4. Cardinal Joseph Ratzinger, *Gospel, Catechesis, Catechism: Sidelights on the Catechism of the Catholic Church* (San Francisco: Ignatius Press, 1997), 25–26.

5. Burrows, 77–78.

Chapter Five: Coming to Know the True God

1. Cynthia Harper and Sara S. McLanahan, "Father Absence and Youth Incarceration," *Journal of Research on Adolescence* 14 (September 2004): 369–397.

2. Cicero Wilson, "Economic Shifts That Will Impact Crime Control and Community Revitalization" in *What Can the Federal Government Do to Decrease Crime and Revitalize Communities?* (The National Institute of Justice and the Executive Office for Weed and Seed, January 1998), 11, https:// www.ncjrs.gov/pdffiles/172210.pdf.

3. P. L. Adams, J. R. Milner, and N. A. Schrepf, *Fatherless Children* (New York: Wiley Press, 1984).

4. John Paul II, Homily in Perth, Australia, November 30, 1986, 4, http://www.vatican.va/holy_father/john_paul_ii/homilies/1986/ documents/hf_jp-ii_hom_19861130_perth-australia_en.html.

Chapter Six: Activating the Gifts of Baptism and Confirmation

1. John Paul II, Regina Caeli, April 2, 1989, 1–3, http://
   www.vatican.va/liturgical_year/pentecost/documents/
   hf_jp-ii_reg_19890402_en.html.

2. John Paul II, Regina Caeli, April 9, 1989, 1, 2, http://
   www.vatican.va/liturgical_year/pentecost/documents/
   hf_jp-ii_reg_19890409_en.html.

3. John Paul II, Regina Caeli, April 16, 1989, 1, 2, http://
   www.vatican.va/liturgical_year/pentecost/documents/
   hf_jp-ii_reg_19890416_en.html.

4. John Paul II, Regina Caeli, May 7, 1989, 1, 2, http://
   www.vatican.va/liturgical_year/pentecost/documents/
   hf_jp-ii_reg_19890507_en.html.

5. John Paul II, Regina Caeli, May 14, 1989, 12, 3, http://
   www.vatican.va/liturgical_year/pentecost/documents/
   hf_jp-ii_reg_19890514_en.html.

6. John Paul II, Regina Caeli, April 23, 1989, 1, 2, http://
   www.vatican.va/liturgical_year/pentecost/documents/
   hf_jp-ii_reg_19890423_en.html.

7. John Paul II, Angelus, May 28, 1989, 1, 2, http://
   www.vatican.va/liturgical_year/pentecost/documents/
   hf_jp-ii_ang_19890528_en.html

8. John Paul II, Angelus, June 11, 1989, 1, 2, http://
   www.vatican.va/liturgical_year/pentecost/documents/
   hf_jp-ii_ang_19890611_en.html.

9. A free download of this booklet is available from Renewal Ministries by clicking on this link: https://www.renewalministries. net/?module=Booklets.

10. "'Nones' on the Rise," Pew Research Forum, last modified October 9, 2012, http://www.pewforum.org/unaffiliated/nones -on-the-rise.aspx.

11. Ibid.

12. Leiva-Merikakis, 37–38.

Chapter Seven: Three More Gifts: Faith, Hope, and Love

1. John Paul II, World Day of Peace 2002, 3, http://www.vatican. va/holy_father/john_paul_ii/messages/peace/documents/ hf_jp-ii_mes_20011211_xxxv-world-day-for-peace_en.html.

2. Philip Yancey, *A Skeptic's Guide to Faith* (Grand Rapids, MI: Zondervan, 2009), 223–224.

Conclusion

1. Andrew Murray, *Absolute Surrender and Other Addresses* (Grand Rapids, MI: Fleming H. Revell Co., 1897), 112–113.

Appendix

1. John Paul II, General Audience, September 6, 1989, http:// www.vatican.va/holy_father/john_paul_ii/audiences/alpha/data/ aud19890906en.html.